Home Office

BUILDING A SAFE, JUST
AND TOLERANT SOCIETY

Life in the United Kingdom

A Journey to Citizenship

The Official Publication

Published on behalf of the
Life in the United Kingdom
Advisory Group

For Life in the UK Test visit **www.lifeintheuktest.gov.uk**

Published by TSO (The Stationery Office) and available from:

Online
www.tsoshop.co.uk

Mail, Telephone, Fax & E-mail
TSO
PO Box 29, Norwich, NR3 1GN
Telephone orders/General enquiries: 0870 600 5522
Fax orders: 0870 600 5533
E-mail: customer.services@tso.co.uk
Textphone 0870 240 3701

TSO Shops
123 Kingsway, London, WC2B 6PQ
020 7242 6393 Fax 020 7242 6394
68-69 Bull Street, Birmingham B4 6AD
0121 236 9696 Fax 0121 236 9699
9-21 Princess Street, Manchester M60 8AS
0161 834 7201 Fax 0161 833 0634
16 Arthur Street, Belfast BT1 4GD
028 9023 8451 Fax 028 9023 5401
18-19 High Street, Cardiff CF10 1PT
029 2039 5548 Fax 029 2038 4347
71 Lothian Road, Edinburgh EH3 9AZ
0870 606 5566 Fax 0870 606 5588

TSO Accredited Agents
(see Yellow Pages)

and through good booksellers

Published with the permission of the Home Office on behalf of Her Majesty's Stationery Office.

ISBN 0-11-341302-5
ISBN 978-0-11-341302-7
Ninth impression 2006

The views and advice contained in this publication are those of the Advisory Group on Life in the United Kingdom and not necessarily those of Her Majesty's Government.

Printed in the United Kingdom
N5389620 C200 7/06

Preface

Becoming a British citizen is a significant life event. The Government intends to make gaining British citizenship meaningful and celebratory rather than simply a bureaucratic process. New citizenship ceremonies will help people mark this important event. We want British citizenship to embrace positively the diversity of background, culture, and faiths that living in modern Britain involves. The Government is also concerned that those who become British citizens should play an active role, both economic and political, in our society, and have a sense of belonging to a wider community. The government has already instituted local welcoming ceremonies at which successful applicants will take the oath of allegiance and a pledge to observe the rules and customs of democratic citizenship. I have asked this new advisory group [under the chairmanship of Sir Bernard Crick], which brings together independent experts in citizenship, integration and education from England, Scotland and Wales, to consider how best to achieve the Government's plans to promote language skills and practical knowledge about the United Kingdom for those seeking to become British citizens.

[The Home Secretary, The Rt. Hon. David Blunkett, MP, 9 September 2002]

We brought in the first ever ceremonies for new citizens, in March this year. I attended the first ever ceremony, in Brent, and like all those who were present I came away with a real sense that this was a powerful way of boosting personal, civic and national pride, challenging society to offer a welcome to those who have positively chosen to take our nationality.

It is important that we underpin this by providing practical support for new arrivals to integrate and to become active citizens, helping all migrants to a better knowledge of our language and our way of life. But the symbolic and celebratory aspect of acquiring British Citizenship must also be underpinned with practical support for new citizens to integrate. The requirement to have an adequate understanding of English needs to mean something, and needs to be supplemented by a level of knowledge of what it means to be a citizen of modern, democratic Britain. And this is where the report of the advisory group has been so valuable. It has offered us not only a well judged analysis of what those core British values are, which I would commend to anyone who hasn't already seen it; it also sets out in practical terms how these new requirements can best be made to work.

As a result, we are developing new types of courses specially suited to the needs of migrants: English language courses which use teaching materials based on the concept of citizenship; and courses specifically about citizenship for people who already have adequate English but need to know more about what it means to live in this country and contribute to the community. Also a handbook or compendium of useful information about this country, compiled by the Advisory Group, will soon be offered to all new immigrants and those taking classes.

[Home Secretary, Speech 7 July 2004]

Contents

If you would like to learn more about how to prepare for the Life in the UK Test visit www.lifeintheuktest.gov.uk

Introduction

Who is this for?

This compendium of information aims primarily to assist teachers of English as a second language, mentors and others helping immigrants to integrate. It will also aid those immigrants, new or old, who have workable English already and who are required to take a citizenship test if, as we hope, they apply for naturalisation as full British citizens with political and legal rights and duties.[1]

In addition to this handbook, the Home Office is providing a shorter document, *Living and Working in Britain*, for new arrivals. This will give essential information in briefer form and will be translated into the main languages of recent arrivals.

If you are an immigrant, welcome to this country. Existing British citizens are well aware that the country needs immigrants, both skilled and unskilled. If you are a teacher, a social worker or voluntary helper working among immigrants, or perhaps just a friend of an individual or family, you may also find this useful.

Most people are welcoming. Britain needs immigrants; otherwise Britain would have a diminishing work force amid a healthy population living longer into retirement and away from the world of work. Government research papers and the statements of Ministers point to the economic advantages to all of a carefully managed migration policy.

---

[1] This publication appears in the name of the independent advisory group set up in 2003 by the Home Secretary whose report was published as *The New and the Old: The Report of the "Life in the United Kingdom" Advisory Group*, September 2003. (Copies can be obtained from the Home Office Social Policy Unit, 6th Floor, Apollo House, Wellesley Road, Croydon CR9 3RR, or on the web at
http://www.ind.homeoffice.gov.uk/ind/en/home/0/reports/life_in_the_uk.html)
This web page will also contain any updates and/or corrections to the Handbook.
The Citizenship Foundation was commissioned to compile and write for the Group's approval the information contained here. Their skills and experience were invaluable. The Employability Forum also co-operated on matters specific to refugees; and some use was made of the data resources of the Citizens Advice Bureau. We have tried hard to check all the facts cited, and we apologise if there are mistakes or important omissions. The Group is solely responsible for opinions and interpretations. However the chairman of the Group, Professor Sir Bernard Crick, wrote and took personal responsibility, after discussion with the others, for the inherently more interpretative sections on "The Making of the United Kingdom" and on "How Britain is Governed".

So this publication is essentially a compendium of useful information helpful to those new arrivals settling in to this country who have "indefinite leave to remain" status or are in the process of obtaining this status. Some sections will be more useful to immigrants who have been here for some time and are now applying or about to apply for citizenship. Many not primarily involved with immigrants may well find basic information here about services, entitlements, rights and duties not easily found elsewhere in one place.

National and regional variations

In one respect this handbook is necessarily incomplete. The United Kingdom contains devolved administrations in Northern Ireland, Scotland and Wales with many important variations in powers, regulations and practices. Important variations are indicated, but not set out in detail.

Immediate needs

Learning the main language of a country is for immigrants anywhere the main priority for integration: to learn enough about the customs of a country to fit in without too much difficulty. To improve one's ability in that language is the path to better employment and to integration generally. The better the command of English, the more one can be aware of and able to exercise the rights and duties of both legal and active citizens.

Language classes are available at different levels in local colleges and centres and the teaching usually contains much useful information relevant to settling in — what is sometimes called "cultural awareness". But it has to be said that most language classes at present involve payment (until you have been in the country three years) and in some areas of the country there may be delays in obtaining access to classes, free or otherwise. Free classes may be available in the future for some categories of new arrivals and people applying for naturalisation. Information on this will be available from local colleges and centres as well as from the Home Office. Some employers now help with such training. Many, unhappily, cannot or do not; but things are changing.

Integration and naturalisation

There are big advantages to becoming a British citizen: the right to a passport and to vote in national elections and for the European Parliament. The belief is common that British passports are more secure than some others; and people who vote play a fuller role in the community, and inevitably are taken more seriously. Many former immigrants and their children are proud to say, "I am now a British citizen".

For a long time the legal qualifications for citizenship were: knowledge of English (or Welsh or Scottish Gaelic, languages spoken in some areas of the United Kingdom); no serious criminal record; and five years actual residence for work permit holders, or three for their dependants (meaning that in each of those years the applicants must have been in the country for a majority of the days of the year). But there was no general assessment of what was meant by knowledge of the language, and it could often be so minimal that employment in an English-speaking environment was hardly possible. Mobility, integration and improvement could suffer.

The Act of 2002, however, requires United Kingdom residents seeking British citizenship to be tested to show "a sufficient knowledge of English, Welsh or Scottish Gaelic" and also "a sufficient knowledge about life in the United Kingdom".

Becoming a British citizen is a significant life event. The Government intends to make gaining British citizenship meaningful and celebratory rather than simply a bureaucratic process. New citizenship ceremonies will help people mark this important event. We want British citizenship to embrace positively the diversity of background, culture and faiths that living in modern Britain involves. The Government is also concerned that those who become British citizens should play an active role, both economic and political, in our society, and have a sense of belonging to a wider community…

The Home Secretary the Rt. Hon. David Blunkett, MP, 9 September 2002

The New and the Old report recommended that for the purposes of naturalisation "sufficient knowledge" of both the language and life in the United Kingdom could be met either by attaining or already being at ESOL Entry Three (English for Speakers of Other Languages) on a first or subsequent assessment and *then* taking a citizenship test; or else by making progress in the lower ESOL language levels which would contain an integral programme of studies about life in the United Kingdom.

ESOL Entry 3 is broadly the ability to hold a conversation on an unexpected topic, that is workable, though not perfect, English. ESOL standards are well established and courses are taught by specialist teachers recognised by the Department for Education and Skills (DfES) in England; and there are similar regimes with equivalent standards in Northern Ireland, Scotland and Wales.

Applicants for naturalisation already settled and new arrivals who want to gain access to ESOL classes will be assessed to discover their existing level of English. They will then have the choice of **either** demonstrating that they are at ESOL Entry 3 already or else preparing themselves, by whatever means, to reach that level; **or else** they must enrol in recognised classes. Those who have reached ESOL Entry 3 without attending classes must then take the short "citizenship test" of knowledge about the United Kingdom. If at all possible new arrivals should begin ESOL classes, or working towards Entry Level 3 by other means, as soon as possible. The results will be registered – "banked" as it were – for when the time comes (five or three years) for the application for naturalisation.

For the current requirements and entitlements, the Home Office Immigration and Nationality Directorate website (www.ind.homeoffice.gov.uk) can be consulted. Or write to Home Office IND, Managed Migration Directorate (Nationality Group), Casework Support Unit, PO Box 12, Liverpool L69 2UX. It is also open to applicants to qualify for citizenship by demonstrating their knowledge of the Welsh or Scottish Gaelic languages. The Immigration and Nationality Directorate are able to provide guidance to anyone who wishes to follow this path.

Note also that the 2002 Act changed the law to require *individual* applications for citizenship. A husband or a wife will no longer by obtaining British citizenship automatically make a citizen of the other. Such spouses will in future have the obligations, entitlements and opportunities of their partners. Human Rights are now seen as individual under both United Kingdom and European law. However, in the case of a citizen's family dependants who may be incapable of taking assessments and tests by reason of age or infirmity, the Home Secretary can exercise discretion to grant citizenship.

Programme of studies

The Life in the United Kingdom advisory group recommended a Programme of Studies that should be followed in language classes whether or not the student has decided as yet to apply for naturalisation. Sections 2 to 8 of this publication set this out: *A Changing Society; Britain Today; British National Institutions; Everyday Needs; Employment; Sources of Help and Information;* and *Knowing the Law.* Those required to take the language classes will only need the shortened version of the Programme of Studies as found in *Welcome to the United Kingdom: what you need to know,* but this handbook will provide more detail when needed for practical purposes. Those taking the citizenship test must be familiar with the sections of this publication, *A Changing Society; Britain Today;* and *How Britain is Governed.*

Some people will know much of this already, others very little. Language teachers always adjust how much they cover in detail to the needs and nature of a particular class. They will teach the sections in whatever depth and order is appropriate to the level and needs of particular classes. In different parts of the country, especially Northern Ireland, Scotland and Wales, different or extra information will need to be conveyed.

The object of the Programme and the assessments required is, we repeat, to be helpful to integration, not to set a rigid task, still less one designed to fail any definite percentage. Hitherto about fifteen per cent of applicants each year fail to obtain citizenship on first application, but almost all of these have failed by not being in the country for the majority of days in each of those five years! British citizenship is not a flag of convenience. No one has any interest in this proportion increasing. If an applicant fails their citizenship application at first go, they can try again when they feel ready, with no limit placed on the number of attempts.

Citizenship ceremonies

The government has already instituted local ceremonies for welcoming new citizens at which successful applicants will take the oath of allegiance and a pledge to observe the rules and customs of democratic citizenship. These ceremonies are popular among immigrants, the local authorities who conduct them and friends and neighbours who may attend.

The first section of this compendium, *The Making of the United Kingdom*, is simply intended as an introduction to give context and background to the rest, as is the similar but shorter section in *Welcome to the United Kingdom*. Neither will form part of the official assessments of progress in language for naturalisation, nor of the citizenship test for those with workable English already who will take the citizenship test. However, some history is essential for understanding the culture of any new country, and can also help in following references in ordinary conversation by British people who themselves may not think they know much history but whose sense of national identity nonetheless echoes past events and beliefs. We British are very fond, for instance, of "the Dunkirk spirit", "the Nelson touch" or "she's a real Florence Nightingale".

Mentoring and integration

This compendium contains information about help obtainable from many kinds of "mentors". Voluntary bodies, charities and faith groups have trained volunteers who can act as friendly advisers on the everyday problems of recent immigrants. They may not be teachers either of language or citizenship skills, but they can be a useful support to both immigrants and their teachers. To seek out or accept a mentor is entirely voluntary. They are not a required part of the programme of studies towards naturalisation. But they can be very helpful. Sometimes mentoring programmes are called "befriending" or simply "community support".

But to integrate into the wider society, improving your employment prospects and skills, you the applicant may need more than the support you should and will probably get from your own ethnic or religious community; but that support needs to give you some understanding of and contacts with other communities, including of course the majority of established inhabitants. There are, for instance, many voluntary bodies you can join – for sociability, to improve your English and your knowledge of the wider society. All this helps integration.

But what is meant by "integration"? Two important statements make clear that integration is extremely important but does not mean complete assimilation.

A former Home Secretary, Roy Jenkins, said in 1966:

[Integration does not mean] the loss by immigrants of their own national characteristics and culture. I do not think we need in this country a "melting pot". It would deprive us of most of the positive benefits of immigration that I believe to be very great indeed. I define integration, therefore, not as a flattening process of assimilation, but as an equal opportunity, accompanied by cultural diversity in an atmosphere of mutual tolerance.

The New and the Old report had this to say:

Many people in the United Kingdom describe themselves as having shared identities, for example, British and Scottish, British and English, British and Indian, British and Bangladeshi, British and African-Caribbean, and there are many other colloquial examples. It should also be recognised that strongly held ethnic and religious identities can remain alongside a British identity but often change or modulate over time…

To be British seems to us to mean that we respect the laws, the elected parliamentary and democratic political structures, traditional values of mutual tolerance, respect for equal rights and mutual concern; and that we give our allegiance to the state (as commonly symbolised in the Crown) in return for its protection. To be British is to respect those over-arching specific institutions, values, beliefs and traditions that bind us all, the different nations and cultures together in peace and in a legal order. For we are all subject to the laws of the land including

Human Rights and Equal Rights legislation, and so our diversities of practice must adhere to these legal frameworks. In all countries at all times the immigrant has sought the protection of the laws in return for giving allegiance to the state. To accommodate the new and the old we all need to live up to the best and generally accepted elements in the political traditions and values of the United Kingdom and to the democratic practices of free citizenship...

So to be British does not mean assimilation into a common culture so that original identities are lost. Assimilation to such a degree has not, after all, not happened for most people in Wales and Scotland, nor historically for Irish and Jewish immigrant communities, nor for smaller communities such as the Poles who once fled from persecution. There is no reason why loss of a distinctive identity within a wider British identity should occur to immigrants from the new Commonwealth or from elsewhere. This is applicable both to the relationships between individuals and between communities, who may all in different ways have made positive contributions to our present way of life. There is wisdom in the old saying "variety is the spice of life"... This is as true for the receiving community as for both new and old arrivals.

1 The making of the United Kingdom

To understand a country well and the character of its inhabitants, some history is needed. We are all influenced more than we imagine by images of the past, true or false, historical or legendary. Any account of British history is, however, whether long or short, an interpretation. No one person would agree with another what to put in, what to leave out, and how to say it. What follows tries to be a coherent if brief narrative of how the different nations came together. However it also mentions some events and persons, which, while not always important parts of that narrative of the making of the British state, yet are often mentioned in books, newspapers, broadcasts and sometimes in conversation and might puzzle new arrivals to our shores

WHAT'S IN A NAME?

The name of our country on British passports is "The United Kingdom of Great Britain and Northern Ireland". This refers to the union of what were once four separate countries: England, Scotland, Wales, and Ireland (though most of Ireland is now independent). Most people, however, say, "Britain" or "Great Britain". Usually "Britain" refers to the mainland and "Great Britain" includes Northern Ireland, and also the Channel Islands and the Isle of Man who have different institutions of government. But even the British can get confused with these different names and usages.

Scots and Welsh if asked, "What is your citizenship?" will correctly say "British", and if asked, "What is your nationality?" they will almost always reply "Scottish" or "Welsh". But the native-born English, outnumbering the others by nine to one, will often give the same answer to both questions, as if his or her nationality as well as citizenship was British. So in the United Kingdom national identity and a strong and proud sense of citizenship are not always the same thing.

"British" conveys those institutions, values, and beliefs that the four nations have in common. These are the laws and customs of the constitution, the crown as a symbol of unity and, for over three centuries, parliamentary and representative government. Originally relatively few people had the vote but nowadays we are a democracy in which almost everyone over the age of eighteen has the right to vote.

However, there are real and valued differences in the broader cultures and ways of life of the four nations. For instance we name poetry, novels and folk song English, Irish, Scottish, or Welsh, rarely if ever "British". Scotland, Wales, and Northern Ireland have recently gained subsidiary parliaments or assemblies with important though limited powers. A common democratic and, with few exceptions, a mutually tolerant politics binds us all together. But apart from politics, the different senses of national identity have created four separate national football teams, and these are recognised in international competitions! Nothing is simple, however: for rugby union the three nations also compete separately but the Republic of Ireland and Northern Ireland combine in one team. In international cricket, England stands or falls alone, though its team may include players from Wales.

EARLY BRITAIN
The Roman conquest

Unity came from conquest. In the beginning of history there were no nations in these Islands, only local tribes. Their great monument was Stonehenge, still standing in what is now Wiltshire. Later came the Celtic tribes, who developed a sophisticated culture and economy.

The Romans, who had conquered and given law and order to the whole Mediterranean world, began to expand into Britain some decades after Julius Caesar had made an exploratory foray into Britain in 55 BC. Not until the following century did they return to conquer and establish control of the entire island except Wales and the north. There was strong opposition from the native inhabitants; one great revolt is still remembered in the name of Boudicca, the Queen of the Iceni tribe in eastern England. To keep out the warlike Celts to the north, the Emperor Hadrian had a wall built across the narrow neck of land between the North Sea and the Irish Channel. Large parts of Hadrian's Wall can still be seen. This division eventually created a kingdom of Scotland.

The fertile lands of Britain led the Romans to call it "the granary of the north". The civilisation they brought with them had a lasting effect. By the time their armies left around 410 AD to defend Rome against invasions of migrating peoples, they had established medical practice, a language of administration and law and had created great public buildings and roads. The routes taken by the main Roman roads are still followed today. Many English words are derived from the Latin language of the Romans. The Romans had no concept of race and little ethnic prejudice. Anyone who obeyed Roman laws and acted like Roman could become a Roman citizen. Before the time of the Emperors Rome had been a republic with a large class of free citizens. The memory of this was never forgotten in the whole of Europe. In Britain a literate administrative and trading class of Romanised Celts emerged, although few among the common people, the peasants, labourers and farmers, could speak Latin.

The coming of the Norsemen

Even before the Romans withdrew, Jutes, Angles and Saxons from Denmark and north Germany had begun to raid across the North Sea and then to invade as settlers seeking better land. The Celts were pushed to the western fringes of Britain, despite resistance perhaps led, at one time, by a Romano-Celtic warlord, who became the mythical King Arthur. Invaders took over eastern Britain, largely ignoring the already decaying Roman culture. The Saxons soon dominated and rival kingdoms were established. But during this time missionaries from Rome spread Christianity across southern Britain, while in the north monks from Ireland converted the land.

In the eighth and ninth centuries, Viking warriors from Denmark and Norway first plundered the coastal lands from the sea and then they came to settle and farm, conquering most of the east of England and the north-east of Scotland. Eventually the kingdom of Wessex, under King Alfred, a scholar, lawgiver, and warrior, united the Saxons and defeated the Danish and Viking armies. But most of the Danes remained, having settled as farmers, been converted to Christianity, and inter-married with the existing population. The Scots and the Irish also came to free themselves from Viking raiders and armies, but again some settlers remained.

The great mixing of peoples had begun. Centuries later Daniel Defoe, the author of *Robinson Crusoe*, called us proudly "the mongrel breed", mocking beliefs that the aristocracy were of pure Norman and the common people of pure Saxon descent.

The Norman Conquest

Saxon rule did not last. A dispute over the inheritance of the crown led William, Duke of Normandy, to sail from France, land on the south coast and defeat King Harold of England at the Battle of Hastings in 1066. That is one date that proverbially "every schoolchild knows", being the last foreign conquest of England.

Unlike the Romans, who governed through local chiefs and leaders (somewhat like the indirect rule that centuries later the British practised in the Indian sub-continent), the Norman aristocracy took complete ownership of all the land and themselves governed with new systems of law and administration. William ordered the first ever census of property values called *The Domesday Book*. Military power depended on the ability to raise taxes. Norman-French became the official language – although Anglo-Saxon continued to be spoken by the common people. They conquered the south of Wales, established a foothold in Ireland, but made no attempt to conquer Scotland. But the Scottish kings and nobility in the lowlands were much influenced by Norman-French culture. There was migration and inter-marrying of noble families so that some great nobles held land on both sides of the border. The highlands and the islands of Scotland remained firmly Celtic or Gaelic in language and tribal culture.

THE MIDDLE AGES

This term is commonly used to cover the period between the Norman Conquest and around 1485, the beginning of the Tudor dynasty when Henry VII came to the throne of England. During this time the English monarchy strove to dominate the Scots, the Welsh, the Irish and to pursue dynastic and territorial ambitions in France.

Times of war

In the thirteenth and fourteenth centuries, the kings of England constantly attempted to control the kings of Scotland by supporting rival claimants to the throne. The English king Edward II received a crushing defeat at the Battle of Bannockburn in 1314 by the Scot, Robert Bruce. The fortunes of war varied but by 1415 England had given up attempts to conquer or control Scotland. By then the largest rebellions of the Welsh had been put down. The English kings destroyed the power of the Welsh princes, the most famous of whom were Owen Glyndowr and Llewellyn ap Gruffydd, by the building of huge castles throughout the land. Edward called his son and heir, the Prince of Wales – a tradition carried on to this day. From 1536 the laws of England were imposed on Wales and the English language was made compulsory for all legal and official purposes. However, Welsh survived among the common people and a bilingual class of small landowners. Language and culture are remarkably resistant to political power.

During the Middle Ages the English kings in the Hundred Years War had claimed the French crown, at first winning great pitched battles, such as Agincourt (celebrated in Shakespeare's play of *Henry V*) and dominating much of France. But they were driven out by continual small-scale actions by the French, almost guerrilla warfare, and eventually by civil war at home.

The origins of Parliament

The origins of our Parliament were in the early Middle Ages. In 1215 the great barons forced a charter of rights from a tyrannical King John. It was known as Magna Carta, the Great Charter. In the nineteenth century historians and statesmen presented it as a charter of liberties for all. But in fact it had little in it for ordinary people, even though centuries later a myth grew up that made it sound like a modern charter of human rights. This was not so but it did show that in England the power of the king was not absolute. He could not tax or wage war without the consent of his fellow peers. The great lawyers said that the king's power was absolute to defend the realm and enforce the laws, but to make or reinterpret laws he had to act politically (in lawyer's Latin, *politicum*): that is to consult and negotiate with powerful others. From this came the origins of Parliament.

The English like to think that theirs is "the mother of parliaments". The English parliament certainly became the most developed in medieval Europe, but it was not unique. Rather it was the survivor of parliaments when elsewhere in Europe in the sixteenth and seventeenth centuries the doctrine of sovereignty arose: that there must always be a single and undivided source of power and law. Monarchs came to claim absolute power: previously they had accepted that power was divided between king, church, and the classes of society and represented in parliament. The English parliament survived because it was more broadly based than others. There was a separate House of Lords – the aristocrats and great landowners – but also a House of Commons of knights, the small landowners, the gentry: a distinctive class in England. Kings found they had more power when they could gain parliamentary consent by influence and persuasion than when they tried to govern alone relying on force. English common law grew up based on precedent and tradition as interpreted by judges who were remarkably independent of the crown. In Scotland there was a broadly similar development except that there were "thrai estates" not two: the clergy sat separately from the lords and the commons. In both countries the churches and the monasteries were the largest owners of land.

Individualism

Almost as important as the growth of Parliament was the growth of individualism. In Saxon and Norman times the land was worked by peasants or serfs tied to a particular landlord by law, custom, and force, and forbidden to change masters. Yet serfs were not slaves; they had some rights in law. They held from their local lord a little land of their own, enough for subsistence; and in return they worked for a fixed number of days, not every day, on his land. The lord protected his people against others in recognition of the oath of allegiance sworn to him by his serfs. This was later called the feudal system. There was an intense sense of community for the common people were rarely able to leave their villages. However, the Black Death or plague of 1348 killed off about a third of the population. Labour became scarce.

Landlords then began to ignore the feudal contracts of service and to poach other men's tenants by offering money. A market for labour grew up. Feudal service gave way to wage labour. Men and women worked harder when working for money. A class of small free-holders emerged, small farmers called "yeomen" who were independent of the great lords. Historians see this as a distinctively English individualism, a cult of personal independence and freedom. The ordinary man saw himself as the embodiment of the nation, loyal to the king more than to any local lord. This was in marked contrast to continental Europe where serfdom or peasants tied to their master's land continued right up to the French Revolution of 1789 and the new ideas triggered by its "Declaration of the Universal Rights of Man". But in England the boundaries and barriers between social classes were already more fluid. People of talent could rise in the world socially as well as economically.

The coming of the modern state

In 1485 Henry VII won the decisive Battle of Bosworth, killing Richard III, and brought an end to a long period of dynastic civil war between two aristocratic clans, those of the Dukes of Lancaster and of the Dukes of York. This period of anarchy was later called the "Wars of the Roses"— the red rose, the symbol of Lancaster, and the white rose of York. The common people were largely unaffected but those of the royal blood ruthlessly murdered any rivals for the throne whom they captured in battle. Henry established the dynasty of the House of Tudor and central administration became greatly strengthened. The Crown's courts established a common justice, law and order throughout the kingdom. The military power of the great nobles was destroyed.

During the Middle Ages an English language and culture had gradually emerged blending Anglo-Saxon and Norman French. Great cathedrals were built, which are nearly all still standing and used – astonishing for their beauty and the skill of their forgotten architects. By three hundred years after the conquest both rulers and ruled began to think of themselves as one nation and spoke the same language. It was in this language that in the last years of the fourteenth century Chaucer published the first literary masterpiece in English, a secular poem of a nominally religious pilgrimage, *The Canterbury Tales*. It was one of the first books to be printed by William Caxton, importing and improving the new and revolutionary technology of the printing press from Germany. The conquerors had become assimilated.

THE EARLY MODERN PERIOD
Religious conflicts

Henry VII suppressed the semi-independent powers and the private armies that had rivalled the crown in the feudal period. That system (but never as systematic as once believed) was one in which the great landlords swore oaths of allegiance to the king and whose tenants swore allegiance to them and their local laws. The medieval king could not command his subjects directly except through their feudal lords. Japan had a similar system to Europe. The ruler's power depended on the size of his own personal estates and on the alliances he could make with his fellow nobles. But Henry VII's son and heir, Henry VIII, "The Great King Harry", established a central administration and enforced a common justice in courts of law throughout the land. Henry VIII also broke from the Church of Rome, defying the authority and spiritual control of the Pope, who had refused to grant him a divorce when the king was desperate for a male heir. The Pope claimed authority over all Christians. But Henry established a Church of England which claimed to be Catholic in doctrine but whose bishops were appointed by the crown. This was the time of the Reformation all over northern Europe. Reformers, calling them themselves Protestants, came to reject the authority of the Pope and his appointed bishops. They read and interpreted the Bible for themselves in their own languages (no longer the Latin of the Church, mysterious to the masses), and different sects reached different conclusions. A belief grew that an individual's conscience was closer to God than the authority of priests and bishops. Gradually the Church of England became more Protestant, although never as extreme as, for a while, in Scotland. Scottish preachers believed that God spoke directly to congregations of believers, who elected their own ministers and rejected the authority of bishops.

Ireland and Scotland

A vital fact of British history is that the Protestant Reformation failed in Ireland. Attempts to impose both Protestantism and English laws governing the inheritance of land led to rebellion of the chieftains and their followers; and through rebellion a new national consciousness arose uniting a tribal society. Many of the original Norman-English settlers remained Catholic and joined the native Irish. Revolts were brutally fought and brutally crushed. In Scotland the Reformation had left the lowlands anxiously divided from the mainly Catholic highlands. Scotland and Ireland suffered terrible civil wars of religion, but not on the scale of Europe where there was ghastly slaughter and persecution between Catholics and Protestants. Wars of religion raged in France in the sixteenth century and the Thirty Years War all over central Europe in the seventeenth century. England was partly protected by the sea from the continental wars, but also by a peculiar religious compromise or "Middle Way".

The Middle Way

Henry VIII's only surviving son, Edward, was strongly Protestant but died in adolescence so his elder half-sister Mary, a devout and militant Catholic, came to the throne with Spanish support. Protestants were persecuted and even burnt at the stake. Catholics had been persecuted during her half-brother Edward's brief reign. When she died childless in 1558 her half-sister Elizabeth inherited the throne, pursuing a moderate Protestantism (soon called Anglicanism) through re-establishing the Church of England. So long as people conformed in behaviour by church attendance, she wanted no questions asked about what people really believed. At times her compromises pleased no one greatly, but she kept the peace. Gradually her popularity rose amid great patriotism, especially after the defeat at sea of the Spanish Armada in 1588. That was a determined attempt to conquer England and to restore the Catholic faith.

The Protestant reformation was more extreme in Scotland. Churches were stripped of all imagery and statues and the nobility expropriated church lands for themselves rather than the relatively orderly seizure by Henry VIII who rewarded trusted courtiers and allies committed to enforcing "the king's peace". In Scotland there was civil war, especially when by the death of a French king in adolescence his young Scottish bride, brought up in the French court as a staunch Catholic, returned to become Queen – Mary Queen of Scots. Rival factions fought to control her in their own interests, not to enforce law and order. She fled to England where her presence was so unwelcome, both as a Catholic and as possible heir to the English throne, that in 1587 Elizabeth was eventually driven to agree to Mary's execution for allegedly plotting against her. Centuries later Mary became a popular legend in Scotland as a good, wise, beautiful, brave, and martyred Queen. Modern Scottish historians only agree that she was beautiful and brave.

Nowadays the period of Elizabeth's reign, called "Elizabethan", is mostly remembered for the great growth of versatility and invention in the use of the wide vocabulary of the English language, drawn from Germanic, French and Latin roots. In theatre and poetry the language reached its height in the genius of Shakespeare, but there were many other poets and writers. Commerce and trade flourished and English seamen and privateers were famed and feared throughout the expanding world of European trade, power, and influence. But when the unmarried and childless Elizabeth, praised by poets as "The Virgin Queen" or "Gloriana", died in 1603 she had no immediate heirs.

Two kingdoms, one king

The English throne passed to her closest relative, James Stuart, the son of the executed Mary Queen of Scots, brought up, however, as a staunch Protestant. He was James VI of Scotland, who then also became James I of England. Wars with England had been frequent, but England had never been able permanently to occupy and hold down Scotland. Attempts to do so had only created a Scottish patriotism in a once divided society. The English were intensely patriotic too, the Spanish and Catholic threat having had a similar effect. Scots were not popular in England and their culture, accents and different English were mocked and insulted. But a foreign king was accepted partly to avoid the risk of civil war between possible English claimants to the crown, and partly because kingdoms were then seen as the property of family dynasties even if alien ones. If James was denied his inheritance, men reasoned whose property would be safe? A foreign ruler was acceptable if chosen by Parliament and able to enforce law and order – "to keep the king's peace". This was far from modern nationalism that rarely accepts alien rule.

James was styled officially "James the First of England and the Sixth of Scotland". Scotland remained an independent kingdom with its own parliament and system of law. He was king in each of two different countries. He wished to create a united kingdom but the two parliaments would have none of it. Union did not come until 1707. He was once mocked for being a learned pedant, and was called "the wisest fool in Christendom". But historians now appreciate his political shrewdness in steering a middle course in both religious and national disputes – except in Ireland. A council of more or less loyal nobility governed Scotland in his name and in his absence.

Ireland: rebellion and plantation

Ireland was overwhelmingly Catholic. It had a Parliament, but Catholics were excluded entirely. England first began invasions of Ireland in 1170 in Norman times. However, over the next four hundred years England succeeded only in occupying securely relatively small amounts of land radiating out from Dublin – the so-called "Pale" or area behind a fence, a paling.

Many of the descendants of the early English conquerors had by the sixteenth century intermarried, adopted Irish customs and spoke Gaelic, the Celtic language, not English as their first tongue. They had remained Catholic.

Following the defeat in 1598 of a widespread rebellion, their traditional leaders fled to France, Italy, or Spain - "the flight of the Earls". So James decided on a policy of "plantation" or colonisation by force in Ulster, the northeastern province of Ireland; not just ruling over the Catholic peasantry, but replacing them. England had grudged the cost of coercing Ireland but had a strategic interest to keep Spain out in the sixteenth and the French in the late seventeenth and throughout the eighteen century. Commercial companies in London were granted the land of dispossessed Catholic rebels. Protestant settlers poured in, mostly from the southwest of Scotland. It was violence and trouble then and trouble for the future. The planters were nearly all small farmers: hard working, independent minded, resistant to central government, fearful of Catholics. The term "plantation" was to be used for the plantations in Virginia and the Carolinas in North America in the next decades.

The King and Parliament

In the last years of Elizabeth's reign and throughout that of James, the Parliament at Westminster became more and more influential. The judges and the lawyers spoke of a balanced constitution: King, Lords, and Commons, mutually dependent on each other and respectful of each other. There was the landed interest but also the growing merchant and commercial interest in the House of Commons. A growing middle class was becoming more articulate and powerful. James's son and successor Charles I lacked his father's political skill. From an early age James was aware how many Scottish kings had died violently. But Charles was tempted by the new doctrines of royal supremacy and absolute sovereignty being preached in Europe. He wanted to tax and rule virtually without Parliament. This provoked Parliament to assert that it was supreme. The time-honoured idea of a balanced constitution temporarily collapsed.

The Great Rebellion

The king recklessly attempted to impose bishops on the congregations of the Presbyterian churches in Scotland. This provoked a Scottish invasion of the north of England. The Parliament at Westminster refused to vote the King "supply" – money for the war. A majority in the Westminster Parliament, probably in the country too, also questioned the spiritual power and ceremonies of the bishops. Many of the bishops' opponents were nicknamed Puritans, perhaps what we might call independent minded Protestants: those who believed in the literal truth of the Bible and that its meanings were clear to all true believers and their preachers. They had no need for priests or bishops to interpret God's word.

The Scots had their way. Throughout lowland Scotland there was a signing of "the Covenant", a mutual pledge, oath or contract to oppose bishops by force if necessary, even if it meant "no king". They believed that the authority of rulers depended on an implicit contract with the people. The king's supporters had claimed that there was "a divine right of kings".

A Catholic rebellion in Ireland should have united King, Puritans in Parliament and the Scots. But Parliament demanded control of the army, fearing that the King might use it against them. He attempted to arrest five parliamentary leaders, bringing armed followers into the House of Commons. They had fled. He asked the Speaker, the chairman of the Commons, where they were and received a famous reply that he had "neither eyes to see nor tongue to speak" except as the House of Commons commanded him. Civil War broke out in 1642.

The Republic or "The Commonwealth"

Four years of fighting resulted in the total defeat of the King's armies. He fled to Scotland but the Scots returned him. He refused to renounce his claims, his royal prerogatives, and he intrigued to regain power. Exasperated that the king would not compromise and that stable government was unlikely with him still alive, Parliament decided in 1649 to execute him. England became for a short time a Republic, calling itself "The Commonwealth of England". Oliver Cromwell, the great general of the parliamentary New Model army (for the first time a citizen army), became leader of the land, a God-fearing dictator, almost a king with the title of Lord Protector.

The Scots had demanded, as the agreed price for their decisive help in the civil war, that their form of Church government be imposed on England. When Cromwell refused, they crowned Charles's son king and invaded England. Cromwell defeated them at the battle of Worcester and then invaded Scotland and destroyed their army totally. He had already turned to Ireland, vigorously and brutally subduing it. His memory is hated to this day by many Catholics in Ireland and praised by Protestants. The English in the nineteenth century came to re-imagine him as the defender of Parliament's rights against the Crown. His statue is prominent outside the House of Commons.

On Cromwell's death, however, there was no agreed system of government or legitimacy. The war had stirred unprecedented religious and political extremism. Democratic and levelling sects began to question the very basis of society – property and social class. But most people became tired of violence and sudden change, frightened of extremism and they longed for stability.

The Restoration

So in 1660 the son of the decapitated King was recalled from exile in France and crowned Charles II. His main ambition was to enjoy the pleasures and luxuries of power in peace. He said he had "no wish to go on my travels again". He got Parliament to pass an Act of Oblivion. All offences committed in the civil war were to be forgotten with no recriminations, except for the few men who had actually signed his father's death warrant. There was an informal toleration of religious and even political dissent, so long as it was limited to sermons and pamphlets and not action. It was a kind of constitutional stalemate or stand off: parliaments could not govern without the King, but the King could not govern without at least occasional parliaments.

Charles was a libertine and a cynic but a shrewd and pragmatic ruler. He did not want his power challenged by Parliament but he did not make any tyrannical use of it. He patronised science. The Royal Society for the Advancement of Science was founded. But he had no legitimate heirs. So on his death the crown of England passed to his brother, James II.

James was an open Catholic, as Charles may have been a secret Catholic. He began to appoint Catholics as officers in the army and he quarrelled bitterly with the judges and tried to govern without Parliament. Powerful groups throughout society became fearful of Catholic domination backed by and under the influence of France. If the restoration of the monarch after the Civil War had proved that England could not be governed without a king, events in 1688 proved that a king could not govern without parliament.

The Bloodless Revolution

In 1688 the great lords conspired together and asked William of Orange, Protestant ruler of part of the Netherlands and married to James's daughter, to invade and be proclaimed king. When William landed there was no resistance. He was welcomed and with his wife, Mary, took over the throne. This change was called the "Glorious Revolution" because bloodless – in England.

But not so in Scotland: pre-emptive action was taken against some of the Catholic and Jacobite tribes (Jacobites were the supporters of James) – the famous Glencoe massacre of the MacDonald clan (or tribe) by the Campbells.

James returned to France, gathered a Catholic army to reclaim the Crown, and landed in Ireland. He was defeated by King William at the Battle of the Boyne in 1690, an event celebrated to this day in song and ceremony by Protestant loyalists in the North. William quickly gained control of the whole of Ireland. Thereafter a policy of conciliation and tolerance was pursued, even if Catholics could not hold public office and there was no formal removal of prohibitions on the Catholic Church. For a century Ireland suffered grievances but was at peace.

STABILITY AND THE GROWTH OF EMPIRE
Constitutional monarchy

The events of 1688 were more than a case of "a bad king" being replaced by "a good king". Those who dominated the parliaments of both England and Scotland had called in William. Many Acts of Parliament in the next decade permanently changed the balance of power between monarch and Parliament. The monarch could dissolve a parliament, but he had then to call a general election. Parliaments had to meet every year and general elections had to take place every seven years (five today). As important as a Bill of Rights was the Mutiny Act. The King had to ask Parliament every year to renew funding for the army and navy. The effect of all this was that the monarch, in order to govern effectively, had to have ministers in a cabinet who could carry a majority of votes in the two Houses of Parliament regularly. So there was constitutional monarchy and then parliamentary government before there was democratic government. It was not democratic because the qualifications for voting were based on the ownership of property, usually at a high level and often centuries out of date. Some constituencies had only a handful of electors and were "pocket boroughs", completely in the pocket of the largest local landowner.

The Act or Treaty of Union

In 1707 came the Act of Union with Scotland, called in Scotland the Treaty of Union. As William and Mary's successor, Queen Anne, had no surviving children, the English government became worried that the Scots could choose a different heir to the throne. Pressure was put on the Scots. The kingdoms of England and of Scotland now became the United Kingdom and under one flag – the Union flag, often called the Union Jack. The members of the old Scottish Parliament surrendered its sovereignty voluntarily, after anxious, sometimes heated debates; but as a treaty between two sovereign bodies, not by reason of an Act of the Westminster Parliament. There was some bribery and corruption, but it was not decisive. And the Scots struck a hard bargain in negotiations. They got for the first time the same rights as the English to trade in the new Empire, without being taxed. The English Empire became the British Empire and Scottish merchants and administrators became especially prominent in it. They kept their own legal system and traditional laws; and their Presbyterian Church (an alliance of the "presbyteries" or small congregations) became established by law. Once again they resisted the authority of the Church of England and its bishops.

The Prime Minister

On the death of Queen Anne, Parliament had turned to her nearest Protestant relative, a German, the Elector of Hanover. George I had to learn English, not very well but just enough to manage. But the founding of this new Hanoverian dynasty (now called the House of Windsor) demonstrated the power of Parliament. King George I (and his three successors who were also called George) still had some influence and power, but they became dependent on ministers and their followers who could control Parliament. The king's friends or the court and church party became nicknamed "Tories" and the nickname "Whigs" was given to followers of the great Lords and their merchant allies who resisted the influence of the crown and defended the liberties of the subject. There emerged the figure of a chief minister, the Prime Minister, then called in the Latin "*primus inter pares*" – first among equals.

The end of the clans

A long and unbroken period of domestic peace began – except for later events in Ireland and a failed rebellion in 1745 by Charles Stuart, the grandson of James the Second, supported mainly by Catholic tribesmen in the Highlands. He had some initial success. As "Bonnie Prince Charlie" he has become now a romantic figure for many Scots, especially in folk songs; but the great majority of Scots either fought against him or anxiously waited on events. In fact he had little interest in being King of Scotland except as a base from which to regain or seize the throne of the United Kingdom. Not all the clans (or tribesmen) had supported him but the clan system was ruthlessly stamped out after their final defeat at Culloden, the last battle fought on the mainland of the United Kingdom.

The clans lost collective ownership of land. Chieftains became landlords by favour of the crown and clansmen became tenants. Many were deported or left for North America as part of "the clearances": the new landlords clearing individual smallholdings or "crofts" to clear the valleys and hillsides for vast herds of sheep. Similar attempts to modernise agriculture and change land tenure in Ireland were less successful and led to constant local conflicts for almost a century and half.

The first British Empire and commerce

Generally the eighteenth century was a time of tolerance and domestic peace. Political philosophers and pamphleteers preached toleration but argued fiercely with each other about issues of the day. The cult of "the gentleman" flourished and spread into many other countries. Social prestige did not depend on birth alone. Men of talent were accepted into "society" if they had property, education, and good manners (even towards one's social inferiors). Toleration of diverse opinions was customary, if they were not too strongly held. Freedom of pen and print became firmly established.

Britain was the first western nation to industrialise. Changes, during the eighteenth century, in farming, metal working and mining techniques and the use of steam power brought greater efficiency and increased production. The first factories were built, villages grew into towns, and many migrated from the countryside into unplanned, unsanitary, and polluted northern and midland cities – what the poet Blake called "the dark satanic mills". Increased production brought increased overseas trade – and with trade, increased colonisation. For over a century and a half Britain was the wealthiest industrial and commercial country in the world. The population expanded rapidly despite considerable emigration to both Canada and the United States – poorer people seeking, as they said, "to better themselves", a phrase with both social and economic meaning

From the mid-sixteenth century onwards, Britain began to extend its power elsewhere. Merchants traded with North America and the West Indies, bringing back sugar, tobacco and other goods for which there was a growing demand. Trade also began with India and what is now Indonesia for spices, tea, and textiles. Naval power came to break the Dutch monopoly of European trade with Indonesia and the Spanish monopoly with the Caribbean.

The slave trade

There was an evil side to this commercial expansion and prosperity, the Atlantic slave trade. Britain and her American colonies became dominant in the slave trade. British ships supplied the southern North American and the Caribbean colonies with men and women seized or bought in West Africa to work on the sugar, cotton, and tobacco plantations. Liverpool, Bristol, and Glasgow flourished on this trade. Despite the value of this human cargo, ten of thousands died in mid-passage chained in the overcrowded holds of the slave ships. There were Arab slavers in East Africa; the Spanish had enslaved the indigenous Indians to work the gold and silver mines of South America; but the English trade became the most famous in Europe, or notorious.

However there were also noticeable numbers of free Africans and escaped slaves living in eighteenth century London, mostly servants but some small craftsmen. A few gained fame in their time as authors, writing graphically of their past and even present troubles. In a famous law case in 1769 Lord Justice Mansfield ruled that an imported and run-away slave, one James Somerset, whose master demanded his return, should go free:

> "The state of slavery is so odious that nothing can be suffered to support it but positive law *[meaning an Act of Parliament, which there was not]*. Whatever inconvenience, therefore, may follow from the decision *[it was argued in court that there over ten thousand owned slaves in Britain – probably an exaggeration]*, I cannot say that the case is allowed or affirmed by the law of England. The air of England is too pure for any slave to breathe. Let the Black go free."

If there were ten thousand others, they would all have been household servants, not slaves in field or factory. They mainly remained household servants, but now free and waged.

Public opinion in Britain, influenced by evangelical Christians like William Wilberforce (1759-1833) and by slave revolts in the West Indies, led to the abolition in 1807 of the slave trade in British ships or from British ports. Wilberforce founded the African Society to agitate for its international abolition. The Emancipation Act of 1833 abolished slavery throughout the empire and the British navy patrolled the Atlantic to stop slave ships of any other nation. It can be endlessly debated whether they were then creating international law or whether they were, in the eyes of other nations, breaking it.

Cultural influences

However for many indigenous peoples in Africa, the Indian subcontinent, and elsewhere, the British Empire often brought more regular, acceptable and impartial systems of law and order than many had experienced under their own rulers, or under alien rulers other than European. The spread of the English language helped unite disparate tribal areas that gradually came to see themselves as nations. Public health, peace, and access to education can mean more to ordinary people than precisely who are their rulers. One legacy of empire was that when nationalism grew most of those who first claimed self-government did so in terms resting heavily on European, on specifically British, ideas of liberty and representative government.

Transitions and transplantations seldom work exactly as intended and are often resented, but India is an interesting example of a national identity gradually emerging amid political institutions that are clearly mutations from the homeland of the imperial era. Indigenous fears that Christianity would replace Moslem and Hindu beliefs were plainly exaggerated, and often the British administrators on the ground, concerned with primarily with civil order and often fascinated by and learned in the ways of local traditions, were not helpful to evangelical missionaries. To some degree the English tolerance of different national cultures in the United Kingdom itself may have influenced the character of their imperial rule in India.

The American War

Throughout the eighteenth century Britain was involved, off and on, with wars against France. The underlying policy that justified war was later called "the balance of power": to prevent any one power from becoming dominant in Europe. This involved colonial wars against the French in India and North America, and the acquisition of new territories.

The British North American colonies had prospered and were mainly self-governing. Immigrants from England and Scotland had gone both to better themselves and to escape from the dominance of great landlords and an established church. The traditions of English liberties were at their height in these colonies. They were mainly lightly governed by what the statesman and political thinker Edmund Burke called "a wise and salutary neglect". Attempts to tax them, to pay for the wars in North American and their defence against the French and the Indian tribes they displaced, led the colonists to demand "no taxation without representation". The refusal of English ministers to compromise "the sovereignty of Parliament" led to rebellion. The colonists at first claimed that they were defending "their rights as Englishmen"; but they soon moved into – or were forced into – claiming independence. The Declaration of Independence asserted universal principles of free government and was welcomed by many reformers in Britain itself and throughout Europe. The teaching of American history in schools was soon to be banned as inflammatory by several European autocracies. The American war was not popular in Britain. It was fought by a British professional army and hired German mercenaries on the one side, and by free and patriotic volunteers on the other.

The second British Empire

French intervention helped the American colonists defeat the British army. After a brief peace, wars with France continued, especially after the French Revolution in 1789. The British navy dominated the seas. Nelson's famous victory at Trafalgar in 1805 over the combined French and Spanish fleets saw the end of any fear of invasion. By 1815, the end of the French Wars, with the defeat of the Emperor Napoleon at Waterloo, Britain claimed territories in Canada, Australia, India, the Caribbean, and in a few parts of Africa. A hundred years later the British Empire had expanded throughout India and included large parts of Africa. Historians call the expansion after American independence "the Second British Empire". It became the largest in the world, with an estimated population of more than 400 million people.

As the Empire developed many people left the United Kingdom to find new opportunities overseas. Large numbers left Britain to settle in South Africa, Canada, Australia, and New Zealand – and also to the United States, that was felt to be close in culture as well as language.

Indeed many emigrants, denied the vote in Britain, favoured "the land of the free" to settlement under the crown. Records suggest that between 1853-1913 as many as thirteen million British citizens left the country.

Industry and political reform

British industry came to lead the world in the nineteenth century. The 1780s had seen a huge boom in canal construction to link the growing factory cities to the ports. They were mainly dug by immigrant Irish labour. However by the early 1830s they were rapidly overtaken by a new technology, the railway engine pioneered by George and Robert Stephenson and then by the great bridge-builder and engineer, Isambard Kingdom Brunel. The railway tracks were laid and the tunnels dug by immigrant Irish labour.

The right to vote

The aristocracy still dominated Parliament but was challenged by the energy and individualism of a commercial and entrepreneurial middle class. The middle class manufacturers created new kinds of domestic goods and comfort for the middle class, although at the same time there was terrible over-crowding and squalor in the working class areas of the growing cities. But most important, the power of the expanding middle class led to Parliament reforming the franchise. The legendary great Reform Act of 1832 was by no means democratic, however. About five percent of the population had a vote before reform and about eight per cent afterwards. The right to vote was still based on possession of property, but it was put on a more uniform basis, abolishing some ancient constituencies with few voters and giving more seats to the cities. This began to shift forever the balance of power from the landed interests to those of the cities, though for a while "masters and men" were politically allied to achieve the abolition of the Corn Laws. These had taxed, in the interests of landlords and farmers, imports of cheap grain from North America to feed the masses. Both the main parties split on the issue, dividing industrial and landed interests.

Universal suffrage

In 1867 working class agitation, coupled with rivalry between the Conservative Party, led by Benjamin Disraeli and the Liberal Party, led by William Gladstone, resulted in the creation of many more seats in Parliament and to the lowering of the property qualifications to vote. Each party vied with the other, if somewhat cautiously, "to woo the masses". The reforms of 1867 were intended to extend the franchise to the skilled and literate working man. Two years later, however, still only a third of men (and women were excluded entirely) were entitled to vote. These numbers were large enough to force the leaders to create party organisations to reach out to the whole country and invite ordinary voters to join. The parties were no longer simply parties in parliament. The party identification began to count far more than the individual personality and influence of the candidates. This was the beginning of something like democratic politics, even if universal suffrage (the right to vote) did not come until all men over twenty-one and women over 30 gained the vote in 1918. Only ten years later did all women get the vote. This was the end of a long period of agitation, including civil disobedience, by the Women's Suffrage Movement.

Imperial uncertainties

Most of the Conservative Party in the late nineteenth century had favoured the expansion of empire while the Liberal Party remained more sceptical or hesitant. Christian missionaries tried to spread their often differing beliefs, often unwanted too, on native peoples; but they also drew attention back home in Britain to poverty and mistreatment. Disraeli, however, had caught the popular imagination by bringing Queen Victoria out of seclusion, following the death of her husband, Albert, to be proclaimed in 1876 as Empress of India. Statues of her appeared almost everywhere. With her many children and austere habits she appeared to symbolise the moral values of family life, what later became called "Victorian values".

However, much educated opinion believed, having studied Latin at school, that the civic freedoms of the ancient Roman republic had collapsed because of imperial over-expansion. A century before, Edmund Burke, the great conservative political thinker, had cried out, "What if the breakers of the law today in India become the makers of the law tomorrow in England?" Liberals claimed that the continuous Afghan and Northwest Frontier wars and General Gordon's death in the Sudan were futile. Conservatives claimed that trade and commerce needed military security and law and order.

The Boer War of 1899-1902 made both viewpoints more intense. British expansion from Cape Province in South Africa to control the gold mines of the Transvaal led to a determined resistance by the two Afrikaner Republics. It took massive manpower resources from throughout the Empire to defeat them. To some imperialists this showed the unity of the Empire, but to others it became the warning, a "writing on the wall" that foretold the eventual collapse of empire. The consequences of the two World Wars and changing political opinions at home were to bring this about.

THE TWENTIETH CENTURY
The First World War

Despite the Boer War, the general mood in Britain was of great optimism, as it was in all Western Europe and in the United States. Even the new Labour Party, born out of discontent at poverty and the class system, believed that they could transform Britain rapidly. Most writers and public figures believed in inevitable progress. A new modern anti-traditional culture of art, literature, and architecture arose alongside this seemingly unstoppable material progress, and even moral progress, as reforming Liberal governments began through graduated income tax to provide unemployment relief and retirement pensions for the poor.

The First World War shattered the great illusion of inevitable progress. The civilised nations of Europe fell into the most terrible and bloody war since the wars of religion three centuries before. All the resources of new technologies, of bureaucratic control and fervid patriotism were used and exploited. Millions were killed and wounded. One battle alone, the British attack on the Somme for four months in 1916 led to about 400,000 British casualties, killed or grievously wounded, and probably the same number of Germans. The whole British Empire was involved in the war at great cost. The Somme was to dominate popular imagination, and after the war recriminations at the generals and at "the older generation" abounded. War memorials became a common sight in nearly every town and village in Britain, usually Christian crosses inscribed with the names of the dead.

The partition of Ireland

In 1916, in the middle of the First World War, an unsuccessful uprising against the British took place in Dublin led by a small group of Irish nationalists. This was quickly put down, but a wave of nationalism was created in Ireland when the leaders were immediately executed under military law, not given a civilian trial. There followed a bitter guerrilla war against the British army and police. In 1921, a peace treaty was signed and a year later, Ireland became partitioned into two parts, the six mainly Protestant counties in the north and the remainder of Ireland in the south. The South gradually asserted its full independence as Eire or the Republic of Ireland. Perhaps the memory of this as well as a growing anti-colonialist public opinion helped speed the end of empire after the Second World War.

The Inter-War Period

The 1920s saw great advances in public housing and a general rise in living standards, until the worldwide "Great Depression" of 1929 created mass unemployment. The new Labour Party formed two governments, but without majorities in Parliament. In 1930 their leader,

Ramsay Macdonald, the Prime Minister, left his party to form a National Government with the Conservatives to deal with the economic crisis. So despite the unemployment, Labour did not form a government with effective power until after the Second World War.

British Prime Ministers in the 1930s failed to understand the territorial ambitions of Hitler, the German dictator and leader of the Nazi Party, and tried to buy him off with concessions (a policy called "appeasement"). Many in Britain blamed the Conservative Prime Minister Stanley Baldwin for complacency and his successor Neville Chamberlain for failing to oppose the territorial expansionist policies of Hitler and the racist policies of his Nazi Party. But the opposition Labour Party was split between those who were, or were almost, pacifists, remembering the slaughter of the First World War, and those who took the Nazi menace seriously. Rearmament was delayed, almost fatally. Although Britain declared war in 1939 when Germany invaded Poland, the Germans conquered Poland, then France, Belgium and the Netherlands. Only when Winston Churchill came to power in 1940 after the fall of Norway did Britain find the war leader it needed so badly.

The Second World War

The Germans prepared to invade Britain but needed to control the air before invasion ships could be launched. But unexpectedly for the Germans' plans, British engineers had developed the Spitfire, a fighter plane of superior design and performance to those of the Germans; and the British invention of radar gave warning of attacks. The "Battle of Britain" was the aerial battle against the Nazi attempt to destroy the Royal Air Force and its bases as preliminary to an invasion; but victory was a close run thing. Winston Churchill was to say of the fighter pilots: "Never in the course of human conflict have so many owed so much to so few".

The German air force switched to nighttime bombing of London and other big cities, famously destroying most of Coventry (then seat of the car industry), and even reaching Belfast and Glasgow. Churchill articulated and stimulated a national spirit of resistance in what he was to call "our finest hour" – that time when "we stood alone" before the United States, when attacked by Japan at Pearl Harbour, entered the war. But in the Far East we were caught off-guard and outnumbered. In Singapore, the huge British garrison and fortress meant to dominate the Far East, quickly fell to the Japanese. For a while they occupied most of Burma and India itself was threatened.

The Second World War truly was a war involving the whole world – except South America, whereas the First World War was mainly a European War in its causes and main location.

But even with final victory, following Japan's fatal mistake of attacking the United States and Hitler's of attacking Russia, British imperial power was ending. The huge involvement of Britain, albeit together with the United States, in the Normandy landings and the invasion of Nazi occupied Europe, was the last great British effort and victory. Prestige had suffered in the Far East. Liberation or self-government movements, which had been growing in India in the 1930s, became strong and successful. The war had exhausted Britain economically and only a few people seriously wished to hang on to India and the other colonies.

POLITICS IN BRITAIN SINCE 1945
The Welfare State

In 1945 the British people had elected a Labour government despite the national admiration for Churchill as war leader. After the high drama of war the British people seemed to want a less spectacular, more reassuring leader, Clement Attlee. Quiet, efficient and seemingly an ordinary man, he met that need. People wanted a break from the past. A free National Health Service was established and the wartime "welfare state", which had guaranteed a minimum standard of living for all, was maintained and enhanced. Unemployment vanished. The railways, the coal mines, gas, water and electricity supply were put under public ownership. The "ordinary man" did a lot. And the break from the past included the colonial past. The Labour Party believed in establishing self-government in the former colonies.

Domestic politics 1951-1979

Despite this Labour was defeated in 1951. They had demanded too much austerity and restraint when Britain was virtually bankrupt after the war, having sold off most of its overseas assets. Food rationing, high taxes on unessential goods and tough monetary controls continued for some years after the war. Despite Britain's diminished economic power, Attlee determined that Britain should secretly develop its own atom bomb so that it could not be ignored in what was otherwise a "bi-polar" world - a two-way bitter rivalry and division of world influence by the USA and the USSR. Europe itself had become divided by what Churchill called "the iron curtain" in "the cold war". And the iron curtain divided Germany too.

The new Conservative governments at first made few changes in the nationalised institutions of Labour's welfare state, content that experienced people should administer them prudently. There was a broad consensus about what was called "a mixed economy", a free market within a framework of public ownership of the key public utilities, transport, and communications industries and a welfare state. Labour under Harold Wilson returned to power from 1964 to 1970 and again from 1974 to1979. There were many educational and employment reforms.

The building of new houses remained a key political issue. But Labour was weakened by constant economic problems of "balance of payments" (importing more than we paid for in exports), inflation and a new instability of international currency exchange rates. Britain was forced to devalue the pound. Shortage of labour led successive post-war governments to encourage immigration, but attitudes and policies were to change (see pp. 43-44).

Many people saw the power of trade unions, a key part of the old Labour movement, as having become too great, an arbitrary restraint on both government and business enterprise. Harold Wilson, the Prime Minister, had constant difficulties with the Left wing of his own party, and they with him. Labour was indeed a coalition - lively but contentious - of socialists, moderate reformers, and trade unions. Ultimately it lost authority by its failure to control large-scale strikes

The Common Market

Meanwhile six nations in devastated post-war Europe had pooled their iron and steel resources through the Treaty of Paris in 1951. By 1957 this had become the Treaty of Rome, in which, led by a reconciliation of West Germany and France, Belgium, Italy, Luxembourg and the Netherlands agreed to form a European Economic Community (EEC). This created a common agricultural policy of subsidies and quotas with powers to harmonise all manner of economic and trade regulations and to open frontiers. A largely consultative European Parliament was established in Strasbourg and a powerful civil service or bureaucracy in Brussels. The motives for integration were not solely economic. Economic integration would also make war between European nations virtually impossible ever again. In future political solutions to conflicts must always be found.

At first Britain did not seek to join. Under Churchill's influence many still believed that the sea-lanes to the United States and the former Empire were crucial. They thought the Commonwealth could form an effective "sterling area". Many resented the idea of surrendering any sovereignty. But the countries of the Commonwealth no longer wished to be tied to Britain's economy. So political leaders came to see the economic advantages of joining the EEC. Britain could no longer stand alone. But twice its application to join was vetoed, once under Harold Macmillan's Conservative government in 1963 and then under Harold Wilson's Labour government in 1967. The French President, General de Gaulle, feared that Britain's influence would be too great and that we were too close to the United States, both culturally and politically.

Finally Edward Heath, a Conservative Prime Minister, negotiated in 1972 Britain's entry into the Common Market. Ireland and Denmark came in at the same time. Since then nearly every country in western Europe has joined and recently many of the countries in Eastern Europe too (following the collapse of Communism and the Russian Empire). The Treaty of Maastricht in 1992 renamed the Economic Community "the European Union" (EU) and increased central powers. This triggered fears by some that the EU was aiming to become a unified state rather than a loose union of convenience of sovereign states, each retaining a veto over important changes.

British parties themselves had always been internally divided on the Europe issue – once whether to join at all; now on the extent of integration. When Harold Wilson returned to power in 1974 the Labour Party was so divided that he had to agree to an unprecedented referendum. Members of his own Cabinet spoke publicly against each other – the famous "agreement to differ". But the voters strongly endorsed continued membership.

The Thatcher Era

The Conservatives won the general election of 1979 and stayed in office until 1997. There followed, under the premiership of Margaret ("Maggie") Thatcher, a period of return to the economic principles of a free market economy. But if she was passionate for free market economics, she loved national sovereignty too; so she had no love for the European Common Market and pursued a pro-American rather than pro-European foreign policy, believing that there was "a special relationship" between the UK and the USA. She privatised the nationalised industries and public services: electricity, gas, water and telephones, and eventually (under her successor John Major) the railways. Parts of the postal system were opened up to competition. People paying rent in municipal housing or "council houses" were subsidised to buy them on favourable terms. The power of the trade unions was challenged and much diminished. The Conservatives turned an old slogan into an effective policy: "Towards a Property Owning Democracy". When they entered office, a majority of the people lived in council houses; but when they left office, a majority owned their own homes. Margaret Thatcher popularised share holding for small investors. Her monetary policies succeeded in controlling inflation but were blamed by some for a massive decline in industry; others however ascribed this mainly to foreign competition. The Thatcher years also saw a great rise in the financial power of the city of London as an international centre for investments, insurance and other financial services.

Local government had its finances cut and powers diminished, reducing its capacity to deal with local problems of poverty and homelessness; free market solutions were regarded as much more likely to be effective in solving the troubles of society.

New Labour

By the time the Conservatives lost power, Labour under a new leader, Tony Blair, had taken on a new name, "New Labour". This was to mark a break from the old policies of public ownership and high taxation to fund public services. New Labour did not attempt to re-nationalise any of the previously public enterprises, or to use taxation in obvious ways to redistribute income. Rather the stress was put on making existing public services more efficient and more accountable, above all education, and the health services. Public and private partnerships were favoured in many of those areas.

Political decisions now increasingly turn on complex issues of the *level* and manner of regulation of public utilities, and the right mix of public and private enterprise, rather than on the old simpler arguments *for* or *against* state or local ownership. At first Blair's personal popularity was great. He seemed to project a new and more popular, classless style in manners and image, if not always as clearly in policy. But people become torn between admiration for strong leadership and distrust of strong government. But in 2003 the Conservatives, under a new leader, Michael Howard, began to offer a more lively, effective and coherent opposition again and to debate new policies.

Strong central control of local government has continued. But New Labour put through devolution legislation creating a Scottish Parliament and a Welsh Assembly which, although stopping short of a federal structure as in the United States, Germany, Australia, Canada or India, gives Scotland substantial powers to legislate and the Welsh Assembly fewer legal and legislative powers but considerable political influence. In Northern Ireland successive British governments have proved unusually innovative in creating new institutional devices to try to get the rival parties to work together.

Today

The government, as all governments do, faces many problems. Some are international arising from differences of opinion on the war in Iraq, whether we are too close or not to the policies of USA rather than the EU, or whether we should be more independent from either. Some problems are domestic: differences about taxation, pensions, law and order, health, education and immigration and asylum policies. In a democracy, of course, leaders can only lead if they can influence or at least do not get too far ahead of public opinion. Leaders need to be followed, but they are followed by people free to change their vote. British voters have become less predictable, more volatile, and not always tied to past party principles or personal loyalties. Britons today seem more inclined than in the past to try to judge the performance of government rather than to vote out of traditional party loyalty. The parties themselves are less fixed in their policies than in the past, and sometimes differences of opinion within each party seem more intense than between the parties.

Britain in the twenty first century is a more mobile and far less class-conscious society than at the beginning of the twentieth century. Almost everybody is far better off in real terms, even if the gap between rich and poor has recently been increasing. The health of people has never been better. Infant mortality is low and people live longer, even if there are some marked differences between social classes.

Britain is also a more pluralistic society both in ethnic and religious composition than a hundred years ago. Post-war immigration now means that nearly ten per cent of the population has a parent or grandparent born outside this country. Most people welcome or at least tacitly accept the economic need for this new wave of diversity. A few do not. There is still racism, even if far less than in the past; and it is actively combated both by opinion and by law and law enforcement. We have been, after all, a multi-national and multi-cultural society for a long time now without losing both our over-arching British identity or our Scottish, Welsh, Irish or English cultural and national identities. New identities and loyalties can fit into this picture of dual identities, and with a common patriotism rather than strident ethic nationalism. It all works reasonably well so long as no identities are asserted as exclusive of the others.

We British may no longer be a dominant world power in either military or financial terms, as in the now distant days of Empire; and yet we seem determined to make our political influence felt on the world stage, not only in the Commonwealth. Our leaders and our press continuously debate whether this means a greater commitment to Europe or to the United States, or whether we can be some kind of bridge between.

2   A changing society

MIGRATION TO BRITAIN

If we go back far enough in time, almost everyone living in Britain today may be seen to have their origins elsewhere. We are a nation of immigrants – able to trace our roots to countries throughout Europe, Russia, the Middle East, Africa, Asia, and the Caribbean. In the past immigrant groups came to invade and to seize land (see pp.18-19). More recently, people have come to Britain to find safety and in search of jobs and a better life.

Britain is proud of its tradition of providing a safe haven for people fleeing persecution and conflict. In the sixteenth and seventeenth centuries, Protestant Huguenots from France came to Britain to escape religious persecution. The terrible famine in Ireland in the mid 1840s led to a surge of migration to the British mainland, where Irish labourers provided much of the workforce for the construction of canals and railways.

Between 1880 -1910, large numbers of Jewish people came to Britain from what are now Poland, Ukraine, and Belarus to escape the violence they faced at home. Unhappily, in the 1930s, fewer were able to leave Germany and central Europe in time to escape the Nazi Holocaust, which claimed the lives of 6 million people.

Migration since 1945

At the end of the Second World War, there was the huge task of rebuilding Britain after six years of war. With not enough people available for work, the British government encouraged workers from other parts of Europe to help with the process of reconstruction. In 1948, the invitation was extended to people in Ireland and the West Indies.

A shortage of labour in Britain continued throughout the 1950s and some UK industries launched advertising campaigns to attract workers from overseas. Centres were set up in the West Indies to recruit bus crews, and textile and engineering firms in the north of England and the Midlands sent agents to find workers in India and Pakistan. For about 25 years people from the West Indies, India, Pakistan, and later Bangladesh, travelled to work and settle in Britain.

In the 1970s, migration from these areas fell after the Government passed new laws restricting immigration to Britain. However, during this period, Britain admitted 28,000 people of Indian origin who had been forced to leave Uganda, and 22,000 refugees from South East Asia. In the 1980s, the largest immigrant groups were from the United States, Australia, South Africa, New Zealand, Hong Kong, Singapore, and Malaysia.

With the fall of the Iron Curtain and the break-up of the Soviet Union in the late 1980s and early 90s, other groups began to come to Britain, seeking a new and safer way of life. Since 1994 there has been a rise in the numbers moving to Britain from Europe, the Middle East, Asia, Africa and the Indian sub-continent, many of whom have sought political asylum. Migrants to Britain, however, face increasingly tighter controls, as the Government attempts to prevent unauthorised immigration and to examine more closely the claims of those seeking asylum.

THE CHANGING ROLE OF WOMEN

In nineteenth century Britain, families were usually large and, in most households, men, women, and children all contributed towards the family wage. Although they were economically very important, women in Britain had fewer rights in law than men. Until 1857, a married woman had no right to divorce her husband, and until 1882 a woman's earnings, along with any property or money she brought to the marriage, automatically belonged to her husband.

In the late nineteenth and early twentieth centuries, an increasing number of women campaigned and demonstrated for greater rights and, in particular, the right to vote. However, the protests and demonstrations were halted during the First World War, as women joined in the war effort and took on a much greater variety of work than they had done before. Women (over the age of 30) were finally given the right to vote and to stand for election for Parliament after the War had ended in 1918. It wasn't until 1928 that women in Britain received voting rights at the same age as men.

Despite these improvements, women still faced discrimination in the workplace. When a woman married, it was quite common for her to be asked to leave work by her employer. Many jobs were closed to women, and women found it very difficult to enter university. The 1960s and 70s saw increasing pressure from women for equal rights and, during this period, laws were passed giving women the right to equal pay and prohibiting employers from discriminating against women because of their sex (see also pp. 111–112).

Women in Britain today

Women in Britain make up 51 per cent of the population, and 45 per cent of the workforce. Girls, as a whole, leave school today with better qualifications than boys, and there are now more women than men at university. Employment opportunities for women now are much greater than they were in the past. Although women continue to be employed in traditionally female areas, such as health care, teaching, secretarial, and sales, there is strong evidence that attitudes are changing and that women are doing a much wider range of work than before.

Research shows that today very few people believe that women in Britain should stay at home and not go out to work. Today, almost three-quarters of women with children of school age are in paid work.

In many households, women continue to have a major share in childcare and housework, but here too there is evidence of greater equality, with fathers taking an increasing role in raising the family and household chores. Despite this progress, many argue that more needs to be done to achieve greater equality between women and men – particularly in the workplace. Women in Britain do not have the same access as men to promotion and better-paid jobs, and the average hourly rate of pay for women is about 20 per cent lower than it is for men.

CHILDREN, FAMILY AND YOUNG PEOPLE

In Britain there are almost 15 million children and young people up to the age of 19. This represents almost a quarter of the UK population. Young people are considered to be a group with their own identity, interests, and fashions that in some ways distinguish them from older people. Generally speaking, once they reach adulthood, children tend to move away from the family home, but this varies from one family and one community to another. Most children in Britain receive weekly pocket money from their parents, and many get more for doing jobs around the house.

Children today in the UK do not play outside the home as much as they did in the past. Home entertainment, such as television, videos, and computers, are seen as part of the reason for this, but so also is an increased concern for children's safety. Incidents of child molestation by strangers are often reported in great detail, but there is no evidence that dangers of this kind are increasing.

As a result of changing attitudes towards divorce and separation, family patterns in Britain have also changed considerably in the last 20 years. Today while 65 per cent of children live with both birth parents, almost 25 per cent live in lone parent families, and 10 per cent live within a stepfamily.

Education

The Government places great importance on the need to assess and test pupils in order to know what they have achieved. Compulsory testing takes place at the ages of seven, eleven and fourteen in England and Scotland (but not in Wales where more informal methods of assessment are favoured). These tests help to give parents a good indication of their children's progress and children know the subjects they are doing well and those that need extra attention.

Most young people take GCSE (General Certificate of Secondary Education) examinations at sixteen, and many take vocational qualifications, A/S and A levels (Advanced levels), at seventeen and eighteen.

One in three young people now move onto higher education after school. The Government aim is to reach one in two. Of those that do, some defer their university entrance by taking a year out. This often includes periods doing voluntary work, travelling overseas, or earning money to pay for fees and living expenses at university (see p. 98).

Work

It is now common for young people to have a part-time job whilst they are still at school. Recent estimates suggest that there are two million children at work at any one time. The most common jobs are newspaper delivery and work in supermarkets and newsagents. Many parents believe that part-time work of this kind helps children to become more independent, as well as providing them (and sometimes their family) with extra income.

It is important to note, however, that the employment of children is strictly controlled by law (see p. 118-119), and that there are concerns for the safety of children who work illegally or are not properly supervised.

Health hazards

Many parents in Britain worry that their children may misuse addictive substances and drugs in some way.

Cigarette consumption in Britain has fallen significantly and now only a minority of the population smoke. Restrictions are planned against smoking in public places. Smoking has declined amongst young people as well as adults, although statistics show that girls smoke more than boys. Tobacco, by law, should not be sold to anyone under the age of 16.

Alcohol abuse is a problem. Although young people below the age of 18 are not allowed by law to buy alcohol (see p.101), there is concern in Britain over the age at which some young people start drinking, and the amount of alcohol that they consume in one session or "binge". Increasing penalties including on-the-spot fines are being introduced to help control this.

Controlled drugs are illegal drugs. It is an offence in Britain to possess, produce, or supply substances such as heroin, cocaine, ecstasy, amphetamines, and cannabis. However, current statistics indicate that half of young adults, and about a third of the population as a whole, have used illegal drugs at one time or another – if sometimes only as an experiment.

There is a well-established link between the use of hard drugs (eg crack cocaine and heroin) and crime, and it is widely accepted that drug misuse carries a huge social and financial cost to the country. Much crime, such as burglary or stealing in the street by threat or violence (called mugging) is associated with wanting money for drugs. The task of finding an effective way of dealing with this problem is an important issue facing British society.

Young people's attitudes and action

Young people in Britain are able to vote in elections from the age of 18 (see p. 73). However, in the 2001 general election, only one in five potential first-time voters actually cast their vote, and there has been a great debate over the reasons for this. Researchers have concluded that one reason is young people's distrust of politicians and the political process.

Although many young people show little interest in party politics, there is strong evidence that they are interested in some specific political *issues*. Those who commonly say they are not interested in politics at all often express strong concern about environmental issues and cruelty to animals.

A survey of the attitudes of young people in England and Wales in 2003 revealed that crime, drugs, war/terrorism, racism, and health were the five most important issues that they felt Britain faced today. The same survey asked young people about their participation in political and community events. It was reported that 86 per cent of young people had taken part in some form of community activity over the past year. 50 per cent had taken part in fund-raising or collecting money for charity.

3   Britain today: a profile

POPULATION

In 2001, the population of the United Kingdom was recorded at just under 59 million people.

UK population 2001

England	49.1 million	83% UK population
Scotland	5.1 million	9% UK population
Wales	2.9 million	5% UK population
N Ireland	1.7 million	3% UK population
Total UK	58.8 million	

Source: National Statistics

More information on the 2001 Census is available from the Government Statistics website, **www.statistics.gov.uk**

Since 1951, the population has grown by 17 per cent. This is lower than the average growth for countries in the European Union (which is 23 per cent), and much smaller than some other countries, such as the USA (80 per cent), and Australia (133 per cent).

The UK birth rate was at an all time low in 2002 and, although it rose slightly in 2003, Britain now has an ageing population. For the first time, people aged 60 and over form a larger part of the population than children under 16. There is also a record number of people aged 85 and over.

Although there has been a general increase in population in the UK over the last 20 years, the growth has not been uniform, and some areas, such as the North East and North West of England have experienced a decline.

The census

A census of the population in Britain has been taken every ten years since 1801 (with the exception of 1941, when Britain was at war). The next census will be in 2011.

When a census takes place, a census form is delivered to households throughout the country, and by law must be completed. The form asks for a lot of information to ensure that official statistics about the population are accurate, but is all completely confidential and anonymous as regards each individual. Only after 100 years can the records be consulted freely.

Ethnic diversity

The largest ethnic minority in Britain are people of Indian descent. These are followed by those of Pakistani descent, of mixed ethnic descent, Black Caribbean descent, Black African descent, and Bangladeshi descent. Together these groups make up 7.9 per cent of the UK population.

Today, about half the members of the African Caribbean, Pakistani, Indian, and Bangladeshi communities were born in Britain. Considerable numbers of people of Chinese, Italian, Greek and Turkish Cypriot, Polish, Australian, Canadian, New Zealand and American descent are also resident within the UK. (See also pp. 98 and 119).

UK population 2001

White	54.2 million	92.0% UK population
Mixed	0.7 million	1.2% UK population
Asian or Asian British		
Indian	1.1 million	1.8% UK population
Pakistani	0.7 million	1.3% UK population
Bangladeshi	0.3 million	0.5% UK population
Other Asian	0.2 million	0.4% UK population
Black or Black British		
Black Caribbean	0.6 million	1.0% UK population
Black African	0.5 million	0.8% UK population
Black Other	0.1 million	0.2% UK population
Chinese	0.2 million	0.4% UK population
Other	0.2 million	0.4% UK population

Source: National Statistics from the 2001 census

Where do people live?

Most members of ethnic minority groups live in England, where they make up 9 per cent of the total population. This compares with 2 per cent each in Wales and Scotland, and less than 1 per cent in Northern Ireland.

45 per cent of the population of ethnic minorities live in the London area, where they comprise 29 per cent of all residents. Most other members of ethnic minorities in Britain live in one of four other areas: the West Midlands, the South East, the North West, and Yorkshire and Humberside.

RELIGION AND TOLERANCE

Everyone in Britain has the right to religious freedom. Although Britain is historically a Christian society, people are usually very tolerant towards the faiths of others and those who have no religious beliefs.

In the 2001 Census, just over 75 per cent of the UK population reported that they had a religion. More than seven people out of ten stated that this was Christian. Nearly three per cent of the population described their religion as Muslim, and one per cent as Hindu. After these, the next largest religious groups are Sikhs, Jews, and Buddhists.

Although many people in Britain have a religious belief, this is not always matched by regular attendance at services. It is estimated that regular church attendance in England is between eight and eleven per cent of the population. Church attendance in Scotland however, although declining, is almost twice the level for England and Wales.

The established church

The Church of England, or Anglican Church as it is also known, came into existence in 1534 (see p.23). The King installed himself as head of the Church, and the title of Supreme Governor has been held by the King or Queen ever since.

The monarch at the coronation is required to swear to maintain the Protestant Religion in the United Kingdom, and heirs to the throne are not allowed to marry anyone who is not Protestant. The Queen or King also has the right to appoint a number of senior church officers, including the Archbishop of Canterbury, who is the head of the Church. In practice however, the Prime Minister makes this selection on the recommendation of a special committee appointed by the Church.

Other Christian groups

Further splits in the Church took place after the Reformation, giving rise to a number of different Protestant denominations. These included the Baptists, Presbyterians, and the Society of Friends (or Quakers), all of which continue today. In the eighteenth century the Methodist movement developed, working in particular amongst poorer members of society.

In Wales today, Baptists and Methodists are the two most widespread denominations. In Scotland there are more than a million members of the Presbyterian Church, the established Church of Scotland, known as the Kirk.

About 10 per cent of the population of Britain are Roman Catholic.

THE REGIONS OF BRITAIN

Britain is a relatively small country. The distance from the north coast of Scotland to the south coast of England is approximately 600 miles (almost 1,000 km), and it is about 320 miles (just over 500 km) across the widest part of England and Wales. However, nowhere in Britain is more than 75 miles (120 km) from the coast.

Many people remark on the great variety in the British landscape. In the space of a few hours it is possible to travel from a major cosmopolitan city to historic sites, old cathedrals, villages, moors and mountains.

Regional differences

In one respect, almost every part of Britain is the same. A common language, national newspapers, radio, and television, and shops with branches throughout the United Kingdom mean that everybody, to some degree, shares a similar culture. However beneath the increasingly standardised appearance of our city centres and suburbs, there are real diversities and cultural differences between different parts of the United Kingdom.

Possibly the two most distinctive areas of Britain are Wales and Scotland. Both have their own language. Welsh is taught in schools and widely spoken in north and west Wales. Gaelic is still spoken in the Highlands and Islands of Scotland. Many people believe that the Welsh and the Scots have a stronger sense of identity and culture than the English – perhaps brought about by their struggle to stay independent (see pp.23-29). The creation of the Assembly for Wales and the Scottish Parliament in 1999 (see pp. 67-68) has led some people to suggest that England needs its own parliament and there is now considerable discussion about what is a distinctive English identity.

Accents are a clear indication of regional differences in Britain. Geordie, Scouse, and Cockney are well-known dialects from Tyneside, Liverpool, and London respectively, but other differences in speech exist in all parts of the country. Scottish and Welsh speech is distinctive, and varies within those two countries. In some areas a person's accent will indicate where they are from, within a distance of twenty miles.

Regional differences also exist in the styles of buildings and the materials used in their construction. Thatched cottages, much less common than they once were, are mainly products of the south, the south-west and east of England. Older buildings are usually made from local stone, giving houses in North Yorkshire, Derbyshire, and many other places a unique appearance.

The industrial legacy of regions also gives rise to distinct styles of architecture. The mill towns of northern England are good examples of this. The insularity of some communities, particularly on the coast and in remote corners of Britain, has meant that their appearance has changed very little in the past 50 years. In contrast, other areas, whose traditional industries have been replaced by others, are almost unrecognisable from what they were a generation ago.

CUSTOMS AND TRADITIONS

Tourist guides commonly paint a view of a rural Britain that is not always recognisable to those who live here. The countryside is regarded by many as "real England", but in fact, the great majority of people live in cities or their suburbs. People's lives in the UK, like many others throughout the world, are a mixture of the old and the new. City dwellers love to visit the countryside. But the abolition of fox hunting, regarded by many city dwellers as long overdue, has been bitterly contested by most country dwellers who see it as a denial of their values and traditions.

Festivals and other traditions continue to exist in all parts of the country, but their existence depends almost entirely on the continued support of those who live in the local community.

Sport

Sport of all kind plays a major part in many people's lives. Football, rugby, and cricket all have a large following, and success on the sporting field is a great source of local and national pride. Major sporting events, such as the Grand National horse race, the Football Association (FA) Cup Final, and the Wimbledon tennis championships, capture the attention of many people in Britain, including those who do not normally follow these sports.

National days

National days are not celebrated in Britain in the same way as they are in a number of other countries. Only in Northern Ireland (and the Republic of Ireland) is St Patrick's Day taken as an official holiday. The greatest celebrations are normally reserved for the New Year and the Christian festivals of Christmas and Easter.

National days

1st March	St David's Day, the national day of Wales
17th March	St Patrick's Day, the national day of both Northern Ireland and the Republic of Ireland
23rd April	St George's Day, the national day of England
30th November	St Andrew's Day, the national day of Scotland

There are also four public holidays a year, called Bank Holidays, when legislation requires banks and most businesses to close. These are of no nationalistic or religious significance.

Religious and traditional festivals

Most religious festivals in Britain are based on the Christian tradition, but also widely recognised are customs and traditions such as Eid ul-Fitr, Divali and Yom Kippur, belonging to other religions. Many of these are explained to children in all the schools as part of their lessons in religious education; and they are celebrated by followers of these faiths in their communities.

The main Christian and traditional festivals

Christmas Day, December 25th, celebrates the birth of Jesus Christ. It is normally seen as a time to be spent at home with one's family. Preparations often begin three or four weeks beforehand, as people decide what presents to buy for close family and friends.

A Christmas tree is usually decorated and installed in the entrance hall or living room, around which presents are placed before they are opened on Christmas Day. Christmas cards are normally sent to family and friends from the beginning of December. Non-Christians usually send cards too, which will often simply say "seasons greetings". Houses are decorated with special Christmas garlands, and sometimes a wreath of holly on the front door. Mistletoe is often hung above doorways, beneath which couples should traditionally kiss. Christmas is both a religious and a secular holiday, celebrated by believers and non-believers alike. Many families attend a church service, either at midnight on Christmas Eve, or on Christmas morning.

Children hang up a long sock, stocking, or pillowcase at the foot of their bed, or around the fireplace for Father Christmas to fill with presents. On Christmas Day families traditionally sit down to a dinner of roast turkey, followed by Christmas pudding – a rich steamed pudding made from suet, dried fruit and spices.

The British Father Christmas is a cheerful old man with a beard, dressed in a red suit trimmed with fur. He travels from an area close to the North Pole on a sledge pulled by reindeer, delivering presents to children. The Father Christmas we have today is often said to be based on folklore that Dutch, German, and Swedish settlers brought to America, although there are a number of other rival theories explaining his origins.

Boxing Day, the 26th December, refers to a time when servants, gardeners, and other trades people used to receive money (a Christmas box) in appreciation for the work they had done throughout the year. Many people still give to postmen.

Boxing Day is a holiday in Britain, where people visit family and friends and continue with Christmas festivities. It is also a popular day for sporting activities - weather permitting.

New Year, January 1st, is celebrated in Britain, as it is in many countries throughout the world. Parties or celebrations begin on New Year's Eve, and when midnight arrives everybody cheers and drinks a toast for good luck in the coming year.

In Scotland , New Year can be a bigger festival than Christmas. Here there is a tradition in many homes of first footing, in which the first visitor of the New Year brings in particular items such as coal, bread and whisky intended to ensure prosperity for the coming year.

In Wales, on the stroke of midnight, the back door is opened to release the Old Year. It is then locked to keep the luck in, and at the last stroke, the front door opened to let in the New Year.

Easter, which takes place in March or April, commemorates the Crucifixion and Resurrection of Jesus Christ, although it is named after the Saxon goddess of spring, Eostre, whose feast took place at the spring equinox. Easter, like Christmas, has become increasingly secular, and often taken as an opportunity for a holiday.

Easter eggs, made from chocolate (traditionally, decorated chicken's eggs) are given as presents, particularly to children, symbolising new life and the coming of spring. Some places hold festivals and fairs on Easter Monday.-

Other traditions

St Valentine's Day, February 14th, is the day when boyfriends, girlfriends, husbands, and wives traditionally exchange cards and presents; cards are unsigned as if from secret admirers.

Mothering Sunday, three weeks before Easter, is a day on which children, young and old, remember their mothers by giving them flowers or chocolates and trying to make their day as easy and enjoyable as possible.

April Fool's Day, April 1st, is the day when people may play jokes on one another – but only until 12 noon. Sometimes even radio, television, and newspapers try to fool people with fake stories and jokes. The tradition is believed to have originated in sixteenth century France.

Guy Fawkes Night, November 5th, commemorates the Gunpowder Plot in 1605 when a small group of Catholics are said to have plotted to kill the King by blowing up the Houses of Parliament. Soldiers arrested Guido (Guy) Fawkes who was allegedly guarding the explosives beneath Parliament. Today he is remembered with fireworks and the burning of a "Guy" on a bonfire.

Remembrance Day, November 11th, keeps alive the memory of those who died in both World Wars and in later conflicts. Many people now hold a two minute silence at 11.00am in remembrance of this, for it was at the eleventh hour, of the eleventh day, of the eleventh month in 1918 that the First World War (often called the Great War) finally came to an end.

The terrible fighting in the fields of Northern France and Flanders devastated the countryside and, in the disturbed earth of the bomb craters, it was the poppy that was one of the first plants to regrow. So this blood-red flower has come to symbolise the sacrifice of those who fall in war.

Today, in the period before Remembrance Day, artificial poppies are sold in shops and on the streets, and many people wear them in their buttonholes in memory of the dead.

4 How Britain is governed

THE WORKING SYSTEM
Parliamentary democracy

The British system of government is a parliamentary democracy. General elections are held at least every five years, and voters in each constituency elect their MP (Member of Parliament) to sit in the House of Commons. Most MPs belong to a political party, and the party with the largest number of MPs in the House of Commons forms the government, with the more senior MPs becoming ministers in charge of departments of state or heads of committees of MPs.

The Prime Minister

The Prime Minister (PM) is the leader of the party in power. He or she appoints (and dismisses) ministers of state, and has the ultimate choice and control over many important public appointments. The Prime Minister's leading ministers form the Cabinet. The Prime Minister used to be called (in the lawyers' Latin of the old days) "*primus inter pares*", first among equals; but nowadays the office has become so powerful that some people liken it to the French or American Presidency, an office directly elected by the people for a fixed term.

However, a Prime Minister who is defeated in an important vote in the House of Commons, or who loses the confidence of the Cabinet, can be removed by their party at any time. This rarely happens, but when it does, the event is dramatic and the effects can be great. For example, Winston Churchill replaced Prime Minister Neville Chamberlain in 1940; and Margaret Thatcher was forced to resign in 1990, when she lost the confidence of her colleagues.

Modern Prime Ministers have their official residence at 10 Downing Street, and have a considerable staff of civil servants and personal advisers. The PM has special advisers for publicity and relations with the press and broadcasting media – all of which adds to the power of the Prime Minister over his or her colleagues. Government statements are usually reported as coming from "Number Ten". If something is directly attributed to the Prime Minister it is of special importance.

The Cabinet

The Cabinet is a small committee of about twenty senior politicians who normally meet weekly to decide the general policies for the Government. Amongst those included in the Cabinet are ministers responsible for the economy (the Chancellor of the Exchequer), law and order and immigration (the Home Secretary), foreign affairs (the Foreign Secretary), education, health, and defence. Cabinet decisions on major matters of policy and law are submitted to Parliament for approval.

THE BRITISH CONSTITUTION

To say that a state has a constitution can mean two different things in different countries. Usually it means a set of written rules governing how laws can be made, and setting out the rights and duties of citizens that can be enforced by a constitutional or supreme court. But sometimes there is no written constitution so that the term simply describes how a state is governed, what are the main institutions of government and the usual conventions observed by the government and the politicians.

The United Kingdom constitution is an unwritten constitution. But although no laws passed by Parliament can be directly challenged by any British court, there are restraints on government. Laws define the maximum length of parliaments, the electoral system, qualifications for citizenship, and the rights of non-citizens. There are the rules and procedures of Parliament itself, and interpretations of laws made by the courts in light of the traditions of the common law.

Sovereignty

A fundamental principle of the British constitution is "the sovereignty of Parliament". But nowadays decisions of the European Union have to be observed because of the treaties that Britain has entered into; and British courts must observe the judgements of the European Court and the new Human Rights Act (see pp.132-133). Textbooks are written on "The British Constitution" and constitutional law, but no one authority will agree fully with another. Some constitutional disputes are highly political – such as what should be the composition and powers of the House of Lords and what is the best system of national and local elections.

Some reformers want a written constitution, as does the third largest party at Westminster, the Liberal -Democrats. But others, including the leaders of the Labour and Conservative parties, value historical continuity coupled with flexibility and have no wish for big issues to be settled by a constitutional court, as in the United States and many other democratic countries. But what holds the unwritten system together is that party leaders observe conventions of political conduct.

Conventions

Conventions and traditions are very important in British political life. For example, the second largest party in the House of Commons not merely opposes the Government but is called "Her Majesty's Loyal Opposition". It has a guaranteed amount of time in Parliament to debate matters of its own choice, and its rights are defended by the Speaker, who chairs proceedings in the House of Commons.

The Leader of the Opposition has offices in Parliament and receives financial support from the Treasury both for his or her office and for the Shadow Cabinet. These are senior members of the main opposition party who 'shadow' Government ministers in different departments. The Leader of the Opposition also has a constitutional status (that is why we use capital letters). He or she stands beside the Prime Minister on formal state occasions, as when the Queen opens Parliament or when wreaths are laid at the Cenotaph in Whitehall on Remembrance Day (see p. 55).

Question Time, when Members of Parliament may ask questions of government ministers, is another parliamentary convention. Questions to the Prime Minister by the Leader of the Opposition are usually lively and combative occasions, often widely reported.

A competitive party system

Under the British system of parliamentary democracy, candidates nominated by political parties, and sometimes individual independent candidates, compete for the votes of the electorate in general elections and by-elections. (By-elections are held to fill a vacancy when an MP resigns or dies in office). The struggle between the parties to influence public opinion, however, is continuous, and takes place not only at election time.

The role of the media

Proceedings in Parliament are now broadcast on digital television and recorded in official reports, known as *Hansard*. Although copies of this are available in large libraries and on the Internet, **www.parliament.uk**, most people receive their information about political issues and events from newspapers, TV, and radio.

In Britain there is a free press - that is, one that is free from direct government control. The owners and editors of most newspapers hold strong political opinions and run campaigns to influence government policy. All newspapers have their own angle in reporting and commenting on political events. Sometimes it is difficult to distinguish fact from opinion. Spokesmen and women of all political parties put their own slant on things too - known today as 'spin'.

In Britain, the law states that political reporting on radio and television must be *balanced*. In practice, this means giving equal time to rival viewpoints. Broadcasters are free to interview politicians in a tough and lively fashion, as long as their opponents are also interviewed and treated in more or less the same way.

During a general election, the main parties are given free time on radio and television to make short party political broadcasts. In citizenship lessons in schools young people are encouraged to read newspapers critically and to follow news and current affairs programmes on radio and television.

THE FORMAL INSTITUTIONS

Government and politics in Britain takes place in the context of mainly traditional institutions, laws and conventions, which ensure the acceptance of electoral or Parliamentary defeat, and peaceful and reasonably tolerant behaviour between political rivals.

The institutional arrangements are a constitutional monarchy, the House of Commons, the House of Lords, the electoral system, the party system and pressure groups, the judiciary, the police, the civil service, local government, and the recent devolved administrations of Scotland, Wales and Northern Ireland, together with a large number of semi-independent agencies set up by the government, nicknamed quangos, and now officially called Non-Departmental Public Bodies.

A constitutional monarchy

Britain has a constitutional monarchy. Others exist in Denmark, Netherlands, Norway, Spain, and Sweden. Under a constitutional monarchy, the powers of the King or Queen are limited by either constitutional law or convention.

In Britain, the Queen or King must accept the decisions of the Cabinet and Parliament. The monarch can express her or his views on government matters privately to the Prime Minister, for example at their weekly "audience", but in all matters of government must follow the Prime Minister's advice. The Queen or King can only, in a famous phrase, "advise, warn, and encourage". There would be a constitutional crisis if the monarch ever spoke out publicly either for or against government policy.

The present Queen has reigned since her father's death in 1952. The heir to the throne is her elder son, the Prince of Wales. He has let his opinions be publicly known on a range of environmental and other matters, but when he becomes King he will be required to act and speak only in a ceremonial manner. Today there are some who argue that modern Britain should become a republic, with an elected President. However, despite public criticisms of some members of the royal family, the monarchy still remains important and popular among most people in Britain today as a symbol of national unity. People distinguish between the persons of the royal family and the institutions they represent.

The Queen is Head of State of the United Kingdom. She is also monarch or head of state, in both a ceremonial and symbolic sense, of most of the countries in the Commonwealth. The Queen has important ceremonial roles in this country, which include the opening and closing of Parliament. Each year at the beginning of a new parliamentary session she reads by tradition "the Queen's speech" from a throne in the House of Lords, stating the Government's policies for the next session. Today, however, these are entirely the views of the Prime Minister and the cabinet.

The monarch also gives the letters of appointment to holders of high office within the Government, the armed forces, and the Church of England, but always on the Prime Minister's advice.

The House of Commons

The House of Commons is the centre of political debate in Britain and the ultimate source of power. It shares the huge Palace of Westminster with the House of Lords. In medieval times, the House of Lords was the more powerful, and so you will still hear some commentators call the Commons, the *Lower House*, and the Lords, the *Upper House*. Today the Commons can always overrule the Lords who can only delay the passage of new laws.

The MPs who sit in the House of Commons are elected from 645 constituencies throughout the UK. They have a number of different responsibilities. They represent everyone in their constituency, they help create and shape new laws, they scrutinise and comment on what the Government is doing, and they provide a forum for debate on important national issues. If you visit the House of Commons you may find few MPs in the main debating chamber. That is because most work is done in committees - scrutinising legislation, investigating administration, or preparing a report on some important issue.

The Speaker

The Speaker of the House of Commons is an ordinary MP, respected on all sides, and elected by fellow MPs. He or she has the important role of keeping order during political debates in a fair and impartial way; of representing the House of Commons on ceremonial occasions; and of ensuring the smooth running of the business of the House.

The Whips

The Whips are small group of MPs, appointed by their party leaders, to ensure discipline and attendance of MPs at voting time in the House of Commons. The Chief Whip commonly attends Cabinet or Shadow Cabinet meetings and will negotiate with the Speaker over the timetable and the order of business.

The House of Lords

The House of Lords is in the middle of big changes. Until relatively recently, the members were all peers of the realm; that is hereditary aristocrats, or people who had been rewarded for their public service - for example in war, the Empire or government. They had no special duty to attend the House of Lords, and many did not do so.

In 1957 a new law was passed, enabling the Prime Minister to appoint peers just for their own lifetime. These Life Peers, as they were known, were to be working peers, and were encouraged to attend debates in the House of Lords on a regular basis. Today those appointed as life peers have normally had a distinguished career in politics, business, law, or some other profession. Recently hereditary peers had their general right to attend the House of Lords removed, but were allowed to elect a small number of themselves to continue to attend.

Life peers continue to be appointed by the Prime Minister although, by convention, always include people nominated by the leaders of the other parties. Senior Bishops of the Church of England are automatically members of the House of Lords, as are most senior judges. Life peers also include members of other Christian denominations and of other faiths – Jewish, Muslim, Hindu, Sikh, or Buddist, as well non-believers and humanists. Today the main role of the House of Lords is to examine in detail and at greater leisure new laws proposed by the House of Commons, and to suggest amendments or changes. In this way the Lords may delay - but not prevent - the passage of new legislation.

The House of Lords also frequently debates issues which the Commons pass over or can find no time for. House of Lords' committees also, from time to time, report on a particular social problem or scrutinise some aspect of the workings of government.

To prevent a government from staying in power without holding an election, the House of Lords has the absolute right to reject any proposed law that would extend the life of a Parliament beyond the statutory five year period. However, if this were ever to happen, the House of Commons could first abolish the House of Lords, who could only delay such an act! This is very unlikely but illustrates how constitutional restraints in the United Kingdom depend more on conventions than on strict law.

The electoral system

Members of the House of Commons (MPs) are elected by a "first past the post" system. The candidate in a constituency who gains more votes than any other is elected, even if he or she does not have a majority of the total votes cast. In the House of Commons, the government is formed by the party gaining the majority of the seats, even if more votes were cast in total for the Opposition.

Under this system, the number of seats going to the winner is always proportionately greater than their total vote. For this reason, some people argue that the system should be changed to one or other form of proportional representation, as in Ireland and most parts of continental Europe. However, neither of the main UK parties favours this, saying that large majorities in the House of Commons guarantee strong and stable government, and that PR (proportional representation) would lead to coalitions and instability.

However, the Scottish Parliament and the Welsh Assembly were both set up with different systems of PR to ensure that they were not completely dominated by a single party, as can happen under a "first past the post" system. Similarly, the use of PR for elections to the Northern Ireland Assembly is intended to stop the Unionist (mainly Protestant) majority of voters from taking all the posts of government, and ensure "power sharing" with the Irish nationalist (overwhelmingly Catholic) parties. In elections for the European Parliament yet another form of PR was adopted to conform more closely to European Union practice.

The party system and pressure groups

The British political system is essentially a party system in the way that decisions are made and elections conducted. There is only a handful of independent MPs or MPs from smaller parties. The main political parties have membership branches in every constituency throughout Britain. Local party organisations select candidates, discuss policy, and canvas the voters in national, local, and European elections. Annual national party conferences are carefully managed and well publicised events, where general party policy is debated, and where local parties can have a significant effect on the Parliamentary leadership.

Public opinion polls have also become very important to the leadership of each party. Party leaders know that they have to persuade and carry large numbers of the electorate, who are not party members, and who in recent years have become less fixed and predictable in their voting habits.

Political party membership in Britain has been declining rapidly in the last few years, perhaps as a consequence of greater consensus between the parties on the main questions of economic management, both seeking the middle ground so that differences of policy and principle are more difficult to perceive; or perhaps because people now, working longer hours and harder, and enjoying for the most part a greater standard of living, can or will give less time to public service. No one knows if this is a temporary or a long-term change. This, combined with falling turn-out in elections, especially among 18-25 year olds, has become a matter of general concern and is widely discussed in the press and in the broadcasting media.

Pressure groups

Pressure groups are organisations that try to influence government policy, either directly or indirectly. There are many such groups in Britain today, and they are an increasingly important part of political life. Generally speaking, ordinary citizens today are more likely to support pressure groups than join a political party. Sometimes people distinguish between "pressure groups" and "lobbies". Lobbies or "interest groups" are seen not as voluntary bodies of ordinary citizens but as the voice of commercial, financial, industrial, trade, or professional organisations.

The judiciary

Since medieval times, judges have prided themselves on being independent of the Crown. Under the British system, judges can never challenge the legality of laws passed by Parliament, but they do interpret legislation and if a law contravenes our human rights, judges can declare it incompatible. The law must then be changed.

As a rule, judges in court normally apply the law in the same way as they have done in the past. This ensures that similar cases are dealt with in a consistent way. However there are times when the circumstances of a case have not arisen before, or when senior judges decide that existing judgements do not reflect modern society. In these situations, by their decisions, judges can create or change the law.

Judges in Britain are appointed by a Government minister, the Lord Chancellor, from nominations put forward by existing judges. The names proposed are those of senior lawyers who are believed to have the ability and judgement to do the job. In the last few years, however, there have been demands - to which the government is responding - that this process should become more transparent, and clearer to members of the press and public. It is also felt that judges should be more representative of the public at large. Many argue that the judges are drawn from too narrow a section of society and that women and members of ethnic minorities are not sufficiently represented.

The police

The police are organised on a local basis, usually with one force for each county. The largest force is the Metropolitan Police, with its headquarters at New Scotland Yard, which serves London. The police have "operational independence" - the Government cannot instruct them to arrest or proceed against any individual. But their administration is controlled by police authorities of elected local councillors and magistrates, and by the role of the Home Secretary. An independent authority investigates serious complaints against the police.

The Civil Service

The Government is serviced by a large number of independent managers and administrators, who have the job of carrying out Government policy. They are known as civil servants.

The key features of the civil service are political neutrality and professionalism. Before the mid-nineteenth century civil servants were appointed by ministers and had to be supporters of the party in power. Civil service reform began in the early 19th century, when the East

India Company governed India. To prevent corruption and favouritism, candidates were required to pass competitive examinations. In the 1860s this system was extended to the Home Civil Service and continues with many modifications today.

Members of the British civil service today are permanent servants of the state, working for whatever party is in power. This neutrality is very important, but is sometimes a difficult balance to strike. Civil servants must warn ministers if they think a policy is impractical or even against the public interest; but must ultimately find a way of putting into practice the policies of the elected Government.

Political party officials tend to do everything they can to put Government policy in a favourable light. Civil servants may find themselves in a dilemma if they think that a minister is being too optimistic about the outcome of a particular policy, or asking them to do things specifically to discredit the Opposition. In the past, commentators suspected that civil servants too easily imposed their departmental policies on new ministers; but now the suspicion is often that civil servants can on occasion be pushed into open support for party policies they think to be either impractical or incompatible with other policies.

A major restraint on civil servants from becoming too politically involved is the knowledge that, if a general election brings another party to power, they will have to work with a new Government - and an entirely different set of aims and policies. When a General Election is pending or taking place, top civil servants study closely the Opposition's policies so that they are ready to serve a new government loyally.

Local government

Towns, cities, and rural areas in Britain are administered by a system of local government or councils, usually referred to as local authorities. Many areas have both district and county councils, although large towns and cities tend to be administered by a single authority, called a borough, metropolitan district, or city council.

Local authorities are responsible for providing a range of community services in their area - such as education, planning, environmental health, passenger transport, the fire service, social services, refuse collection, libraries, and housing. Today local authorities in England and Wales have considerably less control over the organisation of these services than they did in the past.

What local government is required to do is called "mandatory services", as decided by central government. Citizens can take them to court if they do not perform them. But there are also "permissive services", though less than in the past: what they may do if they want to and can afford to do. In England and Wales local authorities may only offer permissive services if empowered to do so by government legislation. However in Scotland, under devolution, local authorities can do anything they are not explicitly forbidden to do. This is a simpler system to understand and operate, but financial constraints make the two systems more similar than might be supposed.

Most of the money for local authority services comes from the Government, provided through taxation. Only about 20 per cent is funded locally through the collection of council tax (see p. 83). There are strict systems of accountability, which determine how local authorities spend their money, and the Government is now beginning to explore how much some local services can be delivered by voluntary community groups. Some see this as diminishing the powers of local government but others see it as a way of involving more ordinary citizens in how their area is run.

Elections for local government councillors are held in May each year. Many - but not all - candidates stand as members of a political party. A few cities in Britain, including London, also have their own elected mayors, with increased powers to manage local affairs. Serving on the local council is still frequently the first step (but less so than in the past) to getting the local party to nominate someone as a candidate for election to the national Parliament or Assembly or to the European Parliament in Strasbourg.

DEVOLVED ADMINISTRATION

In 1997, the Government began a programme of devolving power from central government, with the intention of giving people in Wales and Scotland greater control over matters that directly affect them. Since 1999 there has been an Assembly in Wales, and a Parliament in Scotland, and the Government is now proposing the idea of regional governments in England when there is a clear local demand.

However, policy and laws governing defence, foreign affairs, taxation, and social security remain under the control of the UK Government in London, although these issues may be *debated* in the Welsh Assembly and the Scottish Parliament.

The National Assembly for Wales

The National Assembly for Wales is situated in Cardiff. It has 60 Assembly Members (AMs) and elections are held every four years. Members can speak in either English or Welsh and all its publications are in both languages. The Assembly does not have the power to make separate laws for Wales but it may propose laws for the decision of the UK Parliament in Westminster. However, it does have the power to decide on many other important matters, such as education policy, the environment, health services, transport and local government, where the present laws allow Welsh ministers a great deal of discretion in making detailed regulations.

The Parliament of Scotland

The Parliament of Scotland in Edinburgh arose as the result of a long campaign by people in Scotland for more independence and democratic control. For a long time there had been a devolved administration run by the Scottish Office, but no national elected body. A referendum for a Scottish Parliament, in 1979, did not gain enough support, but when another was held in 1997, the electorate gave a clear "yes" both to establishing a Scottish Parliament and to it having limited powers to vary national income tax.

Today there are 129 Members of the Scottish Parliament (MSPs) in Edinburgh, who are elected by a form of proportional representation. Unlike the Welsh Assembly, the Scottish Parliament may pass legislation on anything not specifically reserved to Westminster (foreign affairs, defence, general economic policy, and social security).

The Scottish Parliament is funded by a grant from the UK Government and can spend it how it chooses. It has the legal power to make small changes in the lower base rate of income tax, which it has not exercised so far, and has adopted its own procedures for debate, the passage of legislation and access to the public – all deliberately different from the traditional ways of Westminster.

The Northern Ireland Assembly

The Northern Ireland Parliament, often called Stormont after the building where it met, was established in 1922, following the division of Ireland after civil war. Protestant political parties, however, dominated the Parliament, and abolished the electoral system of proportional representation that was designed to protect the Catholic minority – a community who faced considerable discrimination in housing and jobs in the public services.

The Government in London paid little attention to these problems until, 50 years later, protests, riots, and a civil disobedience campaign led them to abolish Stormont when reforms failed to materialise. Conflicts increased between Protestant and Catholic groups, the former determined to remain part of the United Kingdom; while the latter determined to achieve unity with the Irish Republic.

There followed many years of communal distrust, violence, and terrorism. But after a negotiated cease-fire by both the main para-military groups – the IRA (the Irish Republican Army), and the UDA (the Ulster Defence Association) – the Good Friday Agreement was signed in 1998 between the main parties and endorsed by the Irish and British governments, working closely together.

Shortly afterwards, the Northern Ireland Assembly was established, with a power-sharing agreement in which the main parties divided the ministerial offices between them. The Assembly has 108 elected members, with powers to decide on matters such as education, agriculture, environment, health, and social services in Northern Ireland.

In view of the political situation in Northern Ireland, the UK government kept the power to suspend the Assembly if the political leaders could no longer agree to work together or if the Assembly was not working in the interests of the people of Northern Ireland. This has happened on a number of occasions.

Non-departmental public bodies

Much of government that affects us all is conducted not directly, but through a multitude of agencies with various degrees of independence. These are organisations that Parliament can create or abolish, or change their powers and roles, but are not a direct part of the civil service. They are sometimes called quangos - quasi-autonomous non-governmental organisations.

A few examples of **non-departmental public bodies**

Trading bodies set up by central government that raise revenue: Her Majesty's Stationery Office (official and semi-official publications), Forestry Commission, National Savings Bank, Crown Estates Commission….

Spending agencies funded by government: Regional Health Authorities, Higher Education Funding Councils, Sports Council, Arts Council, Legal Services Commission, Medical Research Council….

Quasi-judicial and prosecuting bodies: Monopolies and Mergers Commission, Criminal Injuries Compensation Authority, Police Complaints Authority, Crown Prosecution Service….

Statutory Advisory Bodies to Ministers: Gaming Board, Health and Safety Commission, Law Commission, Commission for Racial Equality, Equal Opportunities Commission, Advisory Board on Naturalisation and Integration

Development agencies (many of which are public-private partnerships): Scottish Enterprise, Highlands and Islands Development Board (Scotland), Welsh Development Agency, Rural Development Commission, several regional Urban Development Corporations....

BRITAIN IN EUROPE AND THE WORLD

In addition to Britain's historical and cultural ties with countries throughout Europe, two major developments have occurred since the end of the Second World War in 1945 closely linking Britain to the remainder of Europe.

The Council of Europe

The Council of Europe was created in 1949, and Britain was one of the founder members. It is an organisation with 50 member states, working to protect human rights and seek solutions to problems facing European society today. The Council of Europe has no power to make laws, but does draw up conventions and charters, which states agree to follow. Examples of these are the European Convention on Human Rights (see p.132), measures to trace the assets associated with organised crime, and a directive for education for democratic citizenship in schools.

The European Union

The European Union originated in the period immediately after the Second World War when Belgium, France, Luxembourg, the Netherlands, and West Germany signed an agreement putting all their coal and steel production under the control of a single authority. An important reason for doing this was the belief that co-operation between these states would reduce the likelihood of another European war.

Britain refused to join this group at the beginning and only became part of the European Union (or European Economic Community, as it was then known) in 1973 after twice being vetoed by France. In 2004, ten new member countries joined the EU bringing membership to a total of 25.

The main aim behind the European Union today is for member states to become a single market. To achieve this, measures have gradually been introduced to remove tariff barriers and to help people, goods, and services move freely and easily between member states. This has involved a great deal of regulation being imposed on businesses and consumers, and has not always been popular.

Citizens of a EU member state have the right to travel to any EU country as long as they have a valid passport or identity card. This right may be restricted only for reasons of public health, public order, or public security. They also have the right to work in other EU countries, and must be offered employment under the same conditions as citizens of that state.

The Council of Ministers

The Council of Ministers is one of the most influential bodies in the EU. It is made up of government ministers meeting periodically from each member state with powers to propose new laws and take important decisions about how the EU is run.

The European Commission

Based in Brussels, the European Commission is rather like the civil service of the European Union, taking care of the day to day running of the organisation. One of the important jobs the European Commission is to draft proposals for new EU policies and law.

The European Parliament

The European Parliament meets in Strasbourg in north-eastern France. Each country elects members roughly proportional to its population. Elections for Members of the European Parliament (MEPs) are held every five years.

The Parliament scrutinises and debates the proposals, decisions, and expenditures of the Commission, but does not decide policy. MEPs have the ultimate power to refuse to agree EU expenditure, but have never done so - although they have held it up. Yet the threat has proved effective on several occasions.

European Union law

European Union law is an important source of law in Britain. EU legislation consists mainly of *Regulations* and *Directives*. *Regulations* are specific rules, such as those limiting the hours that drivers of goods vehicles can work, which automatically have the force of law in all EU member states. Regulations override national legislation and must be followed by the courts in each member state.

Directives are general requirements that must be introduced within a set time, but the way in which they are implemented is left to each member state. An example of this is the procedures that must be followed by companies when making staff redundant.

All proposals for new EU laws are examined by a committee of the UK Parliament, which then recommends any changes or amendments to ministers, who will decide whether to try and change or renegotiate them.

The Commonwealth

The Commonwealth arose out of the former British Empire that once included much of Africa and the West Indies, Canada, the Indian sub-continent, Australia and New Zealand. Since 1945, almost all these countries have become independent and together form a loose association called the Commonwealth, with the Crown at its symbolic head.

Only the United Nations is a larger international organisation than the British Commonwealth. The Commonwealth has a membership of 54 states, which together contain 1.7 billion people – 30 per cent of the world's population. Its aims include the development of democracy, good government, and the eradication of poverty, but it has no power over its members other than that of persuasion and only rarely acts together on international issues.

A common language, similarities in culture, and (with some exceptions) mutual recognition of professional qualifications, has greatly assisted the movement of people within the Commonwealth, and had a major effect on migration both to and from Britain.

The United Nations

Britain, like most countries in the world, is a member of the United Nations (UN) - an international organisation, working to prevent war and to maintain international peace and security. Britain is a permanent member of the UN Security Council. The functions of this group include recommending action by the UN in the event of international crises and threats to peace.

Two very important documents produced by the United Nations are the Universal Declaration of Human Rights and the UN Convention on the Rights of the Child. Britain has signed and ratified both of these agreements. Although neither have the force of law, they are important measures by which the behaviour of a state can be judged, and they are increasingly used both in political debate and in legal cases, to reinforce points of law.

THE ORDINARY CITIZEN
The right to vote

How does the ordinary citizen connect to government? As we have seen, full democracy came slowly to Britain. Only in 1928 did both men and women aged 21 and over gain the right to vote. The present voting age of 18 was set in 1969.

Both British born and naturalised citizens have full civic rights and duties (such as jury service), including the right to vote in all elections, as long as they are on the electoral register. Permanent residents who are not citizens have all civil and welfare rights except the right to hold a British passport and a general right to vote.

The electoral register

In order to vote in a parliamentary, local, or European election, you must have your name on the register of electors, known as the electoral register. If you are eligible to vote you may register at any time by contacting your local council election registration office. Voter registration forms are also available, in English, Welsh, and a number of other languages, via the Internet from the Electoral Commission, **www.electoralcommission.org.uk**

However the electoral register is also updated annually and an electoral registration form is sent to all households in September or October each year. The form should be completed according to the instructions, and should include everyone eligible to vote who is resident in the household on 15th October.

By law, a local authority has to make the electoral register available for anyone to look at. The register is held at the local electoral registration office (or council office in England and Wales) and some public buildings, such as libraries (however this is not always possible as new regulations require that any viewing of the electoral register is supervised, and libraries do not always have the necessary resources).

You have the right to have your name placed on the electoral register if you are aged 18 or over and a citizen of the United Kingdom, the Commonwealth, or a European Union member state. Citizens of the United Kingdom, the Commonwealth, and the Irish Republic resident in this country may vote in all public elections. Citizens of EU states, resident in the UK, have the right to vote in all but national parliamentary elections.

Participation

The number of people turning out to vote in parliamentary elections in Britain has been falling for several years, especially amongst the young. In the General Election of 2001, less than half of voters below the age of 25 actually voted. The Government and the political parties are looking for ways in which this trend might be reversed.

Standing for office

Citizens of the United Kingdom, the Irish Republic, or the Commonwealth, aged 21 or over, may stand for public office. However, there are some exceptions, which include peers, members of the armed forces, civil servants, and those found guilty of certain criminal offences.

To become a local councillor, a candidate must have a local connection with the area, through work, by being on the electoral register, or through renting or owning land or property.

This rule, however, does not apply to MPs, MEPs, or to members of the Scottish Parliament, or the Welsh or Northern Ireland Assemblies. Candidates standing for these bodies must pay a deposit of £500, which is not returned if they receive less than five per cent of the vote. The deposit for candidates standing as a Member of the European Parliament is £5,000. This is to discourage frivolous or hopeless candidates, though many still try their luck.

Contacting elected members

All elected members have a duty to serve and represent the interests of their constituents. Contact details of all your representatives and their parties are available from the local library. Those of Assembly Members, MPs, and MEPs are listed in the phone book and Yellow Pages. An MP may be reached either at their constituency office or their office in the House of Commons by letter or phone. The address: House of Commons, Westminster, London SW1A 0AA, tel 020 7219 3000.

Many Assembly Members, MPs, and MEPs hold regular local 'surgeries', often on Saturday mornings. These are generally advertised in the local paper, and allow constituents to call in person to raise matters of concern. You can also find out the name of local MP and get in touch with them by fax through the website, **www.writetothem.com** This service is free.

5   Everyday needs

HOUSING

To buy or to rent? About two thirds of the people in Britain either own, or are in the process of buying, their own home. Most others live in houses or flats that they rent from a private landlord, the local council, or a housing association.

Those people who buy their property almost always pay for it with a special loan called a mortgage, which they must repay, with interest, over a long period of time, usually 25 years. A bank, building society, or estate agent can explain the different types of mortgage that are available, and in particular how much they are likely to cost.

Islamic mortgages

At present, a small, but increasing number of lenders in the UK offer mortgages that do not break Islamic law, which forbids paying or charging interest when borrowing or lending money. Current information is available from High Street banks, building societies, and financial advisers, listed in the Yellow Pages and Thomson Local guides.

Buying a house

Help from a solicitor in buying or selling property is almost essential, especially if the other person is using a solicitor. The system of house purchase is different in Scotland from elsewhere in the UK. A solicitor will again be able to advise you on this (see p. 143). If you are thinking of buying a house or flat, the first place to start is with an estate agent, or in Scotland usually a solicitor, who can give you details of properties for sale in your price range. Estate agents advertise in local papers, they have shops in all towns and cities, and many have websites, with pictures and details of homes for sale.

The estate agent will make an appointment and arrange for you to look at any property that particularly interests you - although don't forget that the estate agent always represents the interests of the seller.

Making an offer

When you find a house or flat that you would like to buy, it is quite acceptable to offer a slightly lower price than the seller is asking. This is one of the few occasions when people in Britain haggle over prices and do not necessarily expect to pay the figure that is being asked. Any offer you make must be said to be "subject to contract" so that you can still withdraw if there are reasons why you cannot complete the purchase.

Solicitor and surveyor

Once you have agreed a price (before is often more prudent), contact a solicitor, who will carry out a number of important legal checks. These include making sure that the person selling the house really does own the property, and checking that there are no plans for new developments, such as road building, that are likely to affect the property that you are intending to buy. The solicitor will also draw up the legal agreement for you to buy the property and deal with the company from which you have obtained the mortgage.

If you have applied for a mortgage to finance your purchase, the bank or building society that is providing the loan will carry out various checks, for their own protection, on the condition of the property. However you will not normally see the results of the survey. It is therefore a good idea to appoint a surveyor of your own to check and report back to you on the condition of the house or flat that you wish to buy. This is useful in bargaining over the price you wish to pay for the property.

Rented accommodation

Rented accommodation in Britain is normally available in one of three ways: from the local authority, from a housing association, and from a private landlord.

National Asylum Support Service

If you have made a claim for asylum in Britain and are being housed by the National Asylum Support Service (NASS), you will have to move and find somewhere else to live if you receive a favourable decision.

You may be given a short period of time to look for a new home, but finding affordable accommodation can be difficult. It is important to ask for advice and help. The local authority is likely to be your first source of advice, see below. In many areas there are also voluntary groups and advice centres that can help you, such as Shelter and the Citizens Advice Bureau. Shelter also runs a free 24-hour emergency helpline for anyone with a housing problem, tel. 0808 800 44 44.

The local authority

Anyone is entitled to apply to be housed by their local authority, often called "the council", although it is important to note that there is a shortage of council accommodation in many areas and a long list of people wanting to be housed.

Although many local authorities have transferred control of their housing stock to housing associations (see below), the housing department of your local authority will still be able to explain your options.

Anyone seeking housing from the local authority must apply to have their name placed on the housing register. The form for this is available from the local authority housing department, and downloadable from the council website. If a person's application to be placed on the housing register is accepted, their needs are assessed, and points awarded according to their circumstances. Priority is given to those living in overcrowded or unsanitary conditions and to families who have young children or where the woman is expecting a baby.

In many areas, people can face a long wait for council accommodation, but applicants have a right to know how their application is progressing and to be given some idea how long they can expect to wait for rehousing.

Housing associations

Housing associations are independent, not-for-profit organisations, providing homes for people in housing need, and are the country's major provider of new homes for rent. Many also run shared ownership schemes to help people who cannot afford to buy their own home outright. There is usually a waiting list for this kind of accommodation. Information on this, and application procedures, is available from the housing department of your local authority offices.

Private landlords

Details of privately rented property can be found through local newspapers, estate agents, and letting agents, who specialise in rented property. The law does not allow estate and letting agencies to charge you for information about housing, or lists of vacancies; they charge the landlord instead.

The rent for a room, house, or flat will vary considerably, depending on the size of the accommodation and the area in which it is located.

Tenancy agreement

When you rent a flat or house you are normally given an agreement to sign by the landlord or agent. This is called a tenancy agreement, sometimes known as a lease, and sets out the conditions that you must follow whilst renting the property.

It is important to check this document very carefully before signing it. For example, it may state that smoking or keeping a pet is not allowed on the property. Breaking rules of this kind can mean that eventually a court may order you to leave.

If parts of the agreement are not clear, it is important to seek help and advice. Free advice on these matters is available from Law Centres and the Citizens Advice Bureau (see p. 122), and the national housing charity Shelter, who operate a 24-hour national housing helpline, tel 0808 800 44 44. Solicitors are also able to help with this kind of problem. Most will charge a fee, but some will offer a free or low-cost interview of up to 30 minutes.

Your tenancy agreement will also include a list of furniture or equipment included in the rental of the property. This is called an inventory. Before you sign the agreement, check the list carefully, and point out anything that is missing or damaged. Keep a copy of your agreement safe so that you can check your rights and duties if there are any problems whilst you are in the property.

Deposit and rent

At the start of your tenancy, you will probably be asked to give the landlord a deposit (often equal to a month's rent) to cover the cost of any damage that you might cause. Always ask for a receipt. This money, less the cost of any damage and unpaid rent for which you are responsible, must be returned to you at the end of the tenancy.

Your rent is fixed at whatever rate you agree with your landlord. If you are in a council property, you must be given at least four weeks' notice of an increase. If you are renting privately your landlord cannot raise your rent during the period of your tenancy without your agreement.

Renewing and ending a tenancy

Your tenancy agreement will be for a specific period of time, quite often six months and, if both sides wish to do so, the agreement can be renewed for a further period of time. However, if you leave before this date, you will almost certainly be required to pay the remainder of the rent that is due.

A landlord cannot force a tenant to leave their home unless the tenant has been given notice to leave in the correct way and generally obtained what is called a possession order from court. However the rules vary according to the type of tenancy. If you receive a notice ending your tenancy it is important to consult an experienced adviser, at a housing advice centre or Citizens Advice Bureau, straight away.

It is a criminal offence for a landlord to use threats or violence against a tenant or to force them to leave without a court order.

Discrimination

It is against the law for a landlord to discriminate against someone looking for accommodation on grounds of their sex, race, nationality, ethnic group, or because they are disabled. However a landlord is allowed to discriminate if he or she (or a close relative) is also going to be sharing the accommodation.

Moving home

If you change accommodation it is possible to have all your mail redirected to your new address for a small fee. You will need to fill in a form obtainable from your local post office, or tel 08457 740 740.

Help!

Housing problems

If you have a housing problem with your landlord, are homeless, or are worried that you may become homeless, it is important to seek advice as soon as possible.

The housing department in your local authority, the Citizens Advice Bureau, or a housing advice centre should all be able to help. So may your local councillor. The housing charity Shelter run a 24 hour housing helpline, tel 0808 800 44 44, and a housing information website, **www.shelternet.org.uk**

Rent and mortgage

If you are out of work or on a low income, you may be able to claim housing benefit, from your local council, to help you pay your rent. You will need to provide your National Insurance number. Further details are available from your local council housing department.

If you have a mortgage and are having difficulties in keeping up with the payments, seek advice and talk to the organisation lending you the money as soon as the problem appears.

Setting up home

Help with the costs of moving and setting up home may also be available from the Social Fund. Staff at a Jobcentre Plus office or Citizens Advice Bureau will advise you.

Examples of help available include:

Community care grant: help for people on income support or income-based Jobseeker's Allowance with the costs of setting up home after a period of homelessness, institutional or residential care.

Budgeting loan: help with the expense of setting up home. Loans of £30 to £1,000 are available; depending on how much can be repaid each week.

Crisis loan: a loan to help people cope with the expense following an emergency or disaster.

Maternity grants: a fixed amount, helping people on a low income to buy clothes and equipment for a baby.

From 2005, Refugee Integration Loans will be introduced, for which new refugees will be able to apply.

Homelessness

If you are homeless, the local authority housing department should be able to help. It has a legal duty to give you advice and help you find somewhere to live. But it will not offer you a place to live unless you are in a category known as *priority need*, that is you have a connection with the area (such as home, work or family links), and have not made yourself intentionally homeless. Being intentionally homeless refers to doing something deliberately that causes you to lose your home.

A person in priority need is someone who is pregnant, or who has dependent children, or is vulnerable in some way, or who has lost their home through something like a fire or flood, or who had to leave their last home because someone was violent towards them.

If you are homeless, or worried about becoming homeless, you should seek advice as soon as possible, see above for details.

SERVICES IN AND FOR THE HOME
Water

Water for drinking and washing is supplied to all homes throughout the UK. There is a charge (known as the water rate) for both this and the removal of used water. Sometimes different companies carry out the supply and removal of water.

When you move in to a new property - whether bought or rented - you should receive a letter addressed to *The Occupier*, giving the name of the company supplying and removing water, the cost, and ways in which you can pay.

Payment is normally made in one lump sum for the year, or in two equal instalments, or by ten monthly payments. The amount that you pay for water normally depends on the size of your property, although many homes have a meter measuring exactly how much water is used. Some water companies give you the option of having a water meter installed.

If you get housing benefit to help you pay the rent you may find that the benefit also covers your water rates. However, it doesn't always do this, and you may have to pay the water rates yourself.

Electricity and gas

All properties in the UK have electricity supplied at 240 volts. Most, but not all, homes are also supplied with gas, which is used for cooking and providing heating and hot water. As soon as you move into a flat or house, it is important to make a note of the electricity and gas meter readings. (Also do the same when you leave.)

If you have a problem with your electricity, gas, or water supplies that needs dealing with immediately, you can ring a 24-hour helpline. Again details are in the Yellow Pages and the phone book, under electricity, gas, or water.

Householders in Britain today can choose from different companies to buy their gas and electricity. The terms and conditions of supply vary, and can be hard to understand. Get advice before signing anything.

To find out the name of your gas supplier contact **Transco**, tel. 0870 608 1524.

You can find out which company supplies electricity to your property already, and get advice on changing supplier, by contacting **Energywatch**, tel 0845 906 0708 and **www.energywatch.org.uk**, who can also give details on changing both gas and electricity suppliers.

Telephone

Today almost all homes in Britain are fitted with a telephone land line, but if you need one installed contact BT (tel 150 442) or your local cable company.

A large number of companies offer land line and mobile telephone services, and it is usually not difficult to change from one telephone provider to another. Advice and information on how to do this is available on the Oftel website, **www.oftel.gov.uk** The pricing schemes for most rival telephone services tend to be quite complicated. It is advisable to read the terms and conditions carefully, to check whether the service offered is what you really want.

Prepaid phonecards are widely available throughout the UK from newsagents, convenience stores, and post offices. They offer large savings, particularly for international calls, but when buying the card you need to give the name of the country that you will be calling, in order to make sure that you get the right one offering the best rate.

Calls can be made from public payphones using cash, phonecards, or credit or debit cards. Call charges on payphones in hotels and private accommodation tend to be high. Emergency calls for police, fire or an ambulance are free by dialling 999 or on mobiles either 999 or 112.

Paying the bills

Information on different ways of paying for all these services is normally given on the reverse of the bill itself. If you have a bank account these bills can be paid by standing order or direct debit. A standing order is an instruction to your bank to make a fixed payment each month. A direct debit permits the supplier, such as the telephone or gas company, to deduct from your bank account either the total amount you owe, or a fixed monthly sum, as agreed by you.

Failure to pay a gas, water, telephone, or electricity bill can result in the service being cut off. A further charge is made when it is reinstalled.

Refuse collection

Every home in Britain has a regular waste collection service. It is provided by the local council and will almost always be made on the same day, or days, each week.

Waste must be put out for collection. In some parts of the country it is collected in plastic bags, in others it is in wheeled bins. In some places you may find that you are supplied with more than one bin, and required to separate paper, glass, metal, or plastic for recycling.

The waste collection service from the home is provided for normal household waste only. Anyone needing to arrange for the collection of large items such as a bed, or to dispose of oil, chemical or medical waste, fridges and freezers, should get in touch with their council who will explain how this should be done. Sometimes there is a charge for this.

Owners of businesses have a legal duty to make proper arrangements for their commercial refuse and waste to be collected. Again the local council can advise on this. It is a criminal offence to dump rubbish in the street, or in the countryside, or on open land, and can result in the person responsible being fined or even sent to prison.

Council tax

Council tax is a property tax charged by local councils, and used to pay for local government services, such as education, police, roads, refuse collection and libraries. The amount payable generally depends on the size and value of the dwelling. The larger the property, the greater the tax. It is important to register for council tax with the local council as soon as you move into a property.

Normally the owner or tenant of the house or flat is responsible for the payment of council tax. Payment may be made in a lump sum each year, by two equal instalments, or by ten instalments from April to January.

Council tax rates are calculated on the basis of two adults permanently sharing the property. If there is just one adult in the dwelling (children under 18 are not included in this calculation), the tax is reduced by 25 per cent. Further reductions are available, for example, if someone living in the property has a disability.

Reductions in council tax are also available to people who have a very low income, or who are receiving Income Support or income-based Jobseeker's Allowance. This is called council tax benefit. Details on this and any matters relating to council tax are available from your local authority offices or the Citizens Advice Bureau.

Buildings and household insurance

If you are buying a house, the company providing the mortgage will insist that you insure the building against fire and theft and other accidental damage. Property insurance for rented accommodation is usually arranged by the owner.

Many people in Britain also insure their possessions against theft, damage, or loss. Insurance can be obtained directly from an insurance company or through a broker, who sells insurance from a number of different companies.

Before signing the agreement, it is important to read the terms and conditions and to make sure that the insurance policy covers your requirements.

Neighbours

Most people find that they get on well with their neighbours by following a few simple rules:
- keep the front clean and rubbish free
- respect the boundaries of people's property
- keep the sound of television, radio, and music to a reasonable level
- greet one another in a friendly way

If you have a problem with a neighbour, the best thing to do at first is to talk to them about it. They may not realise the difficulty. Sometimes it is also helpful to talk to other neighbours, to see if they too are affected.

If the problem cannot be solved in this way, you can talk to your landlord if you live in rented accommodation, or ask for advice from the housing or the environment department at your local authority It is a good idea to keep a record of the events to be able to show when and how often difficulties occur.

Most tenancy agreements, particularly those for local authority or housing association accommodation, require tenants not to be a nuisance towards their neighbours. A person who breaks their tenancy agreement in this way may be taken to court and evicted from their home.

There are a number of organisations, such as Mediation UK, that help neighbours to sort out their differences, without having to take expensive legal action. Trained mediators talk to both sides in the dispute and help them find a solution that they can both accept. These services are usually free. Details are available from local council housing departments, the Citizens Advice Bureau and Mediation UK, tel 0117 904 6661, **www.mediationuk.org.uk**

MONEY AND CREDIT

Although many people in Britain use bank or credit cards to pay for goods that they buy, cash is still an important way of paying for things - especially household goods and food. Banknotes are printed in denominations of £5, £10, £20, and £50 - although shop assistants may be unwilling to accept £50 notes, fearing that they may be forged.

Northern Ireland and Scotland have their own banknotes, although notes issued by the Bank of England are also legal currency. Some banks in Northern Ireland and Scotland issue their own notes, which are also valid all over the United Kingdom.

The euro

The United Kingdom was not amongst the twelve European Union states that adopted the euro as their currency in January 2002. The Government has said that when it decides that joining the euro is in the British interest, it will put the matter to a vote in Parliament and then to a referendum by the British people.

Foreign currency

You can buy or exchange foreign currency at banks, building societies, and large post offices, although in some places you may need to give two or three days notice for particular currencies. Many towns also have money exchange shops or bureaux where you can change money. It is advisable to compare exchange rates and commission charges of a number of bureaux in order to find the best deal.

Banks

More than nine out of ten adults in Britain have a bank account. Many employers pay salaries directly into a bank account. In large towns there are a number of banks to choose from, and if you have time it is a good idea to compare the benefits that each offer.

To open a bank account in Britain you will need to show the bank documents that prove who you are and where you live in the UK. Banks normally accept a passport, immigration document, or driving licence as forms of identification, and a tenancy agreement or household bill (for example, electricity, gas or telephone), containing your name and address. Banks will also accept a letter from someone such as a doctor or a social worker, confirming your name and address.

If you have difficulty providing the right documents, ask the bank to refer you to the person who has the authority to decide on exceptional cases.

Building societies

The first building societies began more than 200 years ago, and were set up to help members buy land and build a house. Today, building societies provide many of the same services as banks. They don't usually have as many branches, but if you are thinking about opening a savings account or applying for a mortgage, you may find that a building society offers the service that you want.

Cash and debit cards

Cash cards allow you to take out money from your bank or building society account through a cash machine. There is usually a daily limit, for example £300, on the amount of money that you can withdraw. You will be given a PIN number (a personal identification number) to use with your cash card. For security reasons, it is important not to let anyone else know what this is.

A debit card (often called Maestro or Delta) enables you to pay for goods without using a cheque or cash. The money is taken directly, and immediately, from your account, and you can use the card as many times as you wish - as long as you have enough money in your account.

If your cash or debit cards are stolen or lost, report the theft to the bank as quickly as you can. Emergency telephone numbers for this purpose are given on bank statements and in the telephone book, under the name of the bank or building society.

Credit and store cards

Although not always accepted in smaller stores, most major credit cards can be used to buy goods from a wide range of shops and businesses. They are commonly used over the telephone and the Internet. However, do this with care. Use only well-known or trusted companies.

If a credit or store card is lost or stolen, the credit card company should be informed immediately.

Credit and store card companies tend to charge high rates of interest to customers who do not pay off their entire bill each month. This can accumulate, and many people in Britain fall badly into debt in this way. Credit cards are a great convenience, but sometimes a great temptation.

Credit and loans

People in Britain are more likely than those in many other countries to borrow money or to pay for things like household goods and holidays by monthly instalments. There are many different ways to obtain a loan or buy goods on credit, but it is important to check very carefully the exact terms and conditions before you sign an agreement.

Many advertisements for credit or loans make the costs of borrowing seem much lower than they really are. If you are uncertain about the terms and conditions of a loan, the Citizens Advice Bureau will be able to explain exactly what these are. A bad credit decision will mean that you end up paying much more for the goods than they really cost and result in a debt that you find very difficult to pay off.

Never agree to a credit agreement over the phone, or with a doorstep seller, unless the caller is responding to a written and signed request made by you.

Being refused credit

Companies giving credit or loans make their decision on the basis of a person's occupation, salary, where they live, and previous credit record. If you are refused credit, you are entitled to ask the reason why.

For a fee, you can check details held on you by credit reference agencies. The Citizens Advice Bureau can explain how to do this and will, if you wish, help you with the process.

Insurance

Many people take out insurance, protecting themselves and their property against unexpected loss or mishap. If you take out a mortgage to buy or improve property, the bank or mortgage company will require you to keep the property fully insured. As well as insuring property and household items (see p. 84), many also take out insurance for the loss of items such as credit cards or mobile phones. If you go on holiday abroad, it is a good idea to have insurance for the loss of your luggage or unexpected medical bills. If you drive a car or motorcycle, you must have insurance by law (see p. 105).

Buying insurance

There are two ways of obtaining insurance. You can either deal directly with the company, or go through a broker. Most large insurance companies have offices in major towns and cities. Their number will be in the Yellow Pages, Thomson Local guide, or phone book. You can often deal directly with them and arrange your insurance cover by phone.

Insurance brokers are agents who help you choose what kind of insurance and which company, and they will arrange the policy for you. They don't usually charge you directly for this, but make their money from the insurance company that you decide to use.

All information you give to the insurance company must be as accurate as possible. If it is not, or you withhold information that could be relevant, your insurance policy will be invalid.

Social security

Britain has a system of social security that aims to provide a safety net to ensure that the living standards of UK citizens do not fall below a minimum level.

One of the main features of the system is the payment of financial "welfare" benefits to people who do not have enough money to live on. The arrangements are complex: there are detailed rules and some benefits depend on having made previous National Insurance contributions (see p. 114). Payments can be claimed in a variety of circumstances, which include those of people who are on a low income, are looking for work, are unable to work, have disabilities and older people.

Guides to benefits are available free from Citizens Advice Bureau, Jobcentre Plus offices, libraries, and post offices.

HEALTH
The National Health Service

The National Health Service (usually called the NHS) was set up in 1948, and is one of the largest organisations in Europe. It tries to provide all citizens with the highest level of medical care. Treatment is free.

Finding a doctor

Family doctors in Britain are known as General Practitioners, and usually called GPs. They often work together in a group practice, normally made up of at least four or five doctors. You may find this described as a Primary Health Care Centre.

Your GP is responsible, at least at first, for arranging almost all the treatment that you receive. This can cover a wide range of problems, and include mental as well as physical illnesses. Only your GP can arrange for you to see a specialist in hospital - although in a genuine emergency, such as a sudden injury or illness, you can attend an NHS hospital without a GP's letter, by going to the hospital's Accident and Emergency department.

Patients with particular needs, such as those who may be survivors of torture, may receive specialist help from organisations like the Medical Foundation for the Care of Victims of Torture. If it is appropriate, your doctor (or solicitor) would make the arrangements for a consultation.

A list of local GPs is available from libraries, main post offices, the tourist information office, the Citizens Advice Bureau and the local Health Authority. You can also ask friends or neighbours for the name of a local doctor that they would recommend.

Registration

It is important to look for a doctor soon after you move into a new area. Don't wait until you are ill. If you telephone the surgery or health centre beforehand, you can check the procedure for registration. Normally you will need a medical card to register with a doctor. If you don't have one, the doctor's receptionist will give you a form to complete and send to the local health authority, who will then supply you with a medical card.

You may at this stage also wish to check whether the practice meets your personal needs. For example, is there a female doctor available? What languages do the doctors speak? Do the doctors offer contraceptive or maternity services?

Some doctors have a very full caseload and are unable to accept new patients. Patients are not always given the first doctor of their choice. If you are unable to find a GP who will accept you, you can ask the local health authority to find a doctor for you.

All patients registering with a new GP are entitled to a free health check.

Using your doctor

You will need to make an appointment to see your doctor, which you can arrange by phone or in person. Sometimes you will have to wait several days before you can see the doctor of your choice. If you or your child needs immediate medical attention ask for an urgent appointment.

Patients are expected to be at the surgery several minutes before the time of their appointment, and to telephone the surgery well in advance if they are unable to keep an appointment. It is important to tell the doctor everything you can, and to answer all questions honestly - even if you find them embarrassing. Do not diagnose yourself with the name of a disease or complaint. Just explain the symptoms. If the doctor says something that you do not understand, ask for it to be explained again.

If you have language difficulties it is always wise to take someone with you who is able to interpret or translate for you. If this is not possible, either you or a friend should explain to the doctor's receptionist when the appointment is made that the services of an interpreter will be required. The doctor will then make special arrangements for someone to be available. In view of the time and cost that this involves, it is important that the appointment is kept.

GPs are also able to visit patients at home, but the huge demand on their time, means that doctors always give priority to those patients who are unable to travel to the surgery. Nurses often deal with simpler procedures.

If you call the doctor outside normal working hours, you will be asked a number of questions to assess the seriousness of your case and then told if and when a doctor will be able to come out to see you. You may be advised to go instead to the nearest hospital accident and emergency (A & E) department.

Confidentiality

Everything you say to your doctor is treated in confidence, and cannot be passed on to anyone else without your permission.

If you feel unwell

There are a number of things that you can do if you or your child feels unwell.

For information or advice • ask your local pharmacist or chemist, or
• speak to a nurse by telephoning **NHS Direct**, or use **NHS Direct Online**.

For urgent medical treatment • contact your GP, or
• go to your nearest hospital with an accident and emergency department, or
• call 999 for an ambulance, if you are unable to get to hospital yourself. Calls are free.
Do NOT use this service if it is not a real emergency.

To see a doctor or nurse • make an appointment to see your GP or a nurse working in the practice, or
• visit an **NHS walk-in centre**.

NHS Direct is a 24-hour nurse and health information service providing confidential information on particular health conditions and what to do if you are feeling ill, tel 0845 46 47. You may ask for an interpreter to provide advice in your own language.

NHS Direct Online is a website providing information about health services and a variety of medical conditions and treatments, **www.nhsdirect.nhs.uk**

NHS walk-in centres provide treatment for minor injuries and illnesses seven days a week. You don't need an appointment and will be seen by an experienced NHS nurse. There are centres in many towns and cities. For details of the nearest centre call NHS Direct, tel 0845 46 47, or visit the National Health Service website, www.nhs.uk, and click on "local NHS services".

Charges

Treatment from your GP is free, but charges are made for most prescriptions and for certain services, such as vaccinations for going abroad.

Prescriptions

If the doctor decides to prescribe medication for your condition you will be given a prescription to take to the local pharmacy or chemist.

Prescriptions are free for anyone who is

- under 16 years of age (or 25 years of age in Wales)
- under 19 and in full-time education
- aged 60 or over
- pregnant, or has had a baby in the last 12 months
- suffering from a specified medical condition
- receiving Income Support, income-based Jobseeker's Allowance, Working Families or Disabilities Tax Credit.

Going in to hospital

If your doctor sends you to hospital for minor tests, you will generally be asked to attend the Out Patients Department, or admitted as a Day Patient if the procedure is lengthier. If you are to stay overnight or longer, as an In Patient, you will be expected to take with you personal items, such as a towel, night-clothes, washing kit, and a dressing gown, but the hospital will provide all meals during your stay. Further information and advice about going in to hospital is available from Customer Services or the Patient Advice and Liaison Service (PALS) at the hospital concerned.

Most hospitals have set visiting hours during which visits to patients may be made. If you can only visit someone outside these hours, speak to the senior nurse on duty and ask if special arrangements can be made. There is often a limit to the number of visitors that each patient may have at one time.

Dentists

You can obtain the names of dentists by asking your friends or by making enquiries at the local library, the Citizens Advice Bureau, and through NHS Direct, tel 0845 46 47, and **www.nhsdirect.nhs.uk** In some parts of the country there are what are known as dental access centres, where patients can receive routine and emergency treatment. Details are available from NHS Direct.

Charges

Free treatment is available to certain groups of people. These include those under 18 years of age, those who are pregnant, and those who have given birth within the last twelve months. Free NHS treatment is also available to anyone if they or their partner receives Income Support, Income-based Jobseeker's Allowance, or Pension Credit guarantee credit. In Wales, free dental examinations are available to anyone under 25 or over 60.

Most people not in the above categories are charged for most dental treatment, and private dentists will generally charge more than those working for the National Health Service. Before starting treatment a dentist should explain the work that he or she intends to carry out and what it will cost; if he or she does not, you must ask.

Opticians

Sight tests are free for children and some young people, for people aged 60 or over, for those with particular eye conditions, and for people receiving certain benefits. Help with the cost of glasses is also available to people in these groups. For more details contact the Citizens Advice Bureau.

Pregnancy

If you are expecting a baby you are able to receive services from your GP and from a midwife, based in either a hospital or local health centre. Not all GPs provide maternity services, and you may wish to register with another GP for your care during pregnancy.

Childbirth in Britain usually takes place in hospital. Doctors often discourage mothers from having their baby at home - particularly if it is their first child - to reduce the risk of possible complications.

Today, in Britain, it is quite common for a father to attend the birth of his child. However he does not have to be present if either he or the mother does not want him to be there.

Registering a birth

Your baby's birth must be registered with the Registrar of Births Marriages and Deaths within six weeks of the birth. The address of your local Registration Office is in the phone book.

The birth can be registered by either parent if they are married, but only by the mother if they are not. If unmarried parents want both their names to appear on their child's birth certificate, they must both be present when the child is registered.

Information on maternity services in your area can be obtained from your local health authority, a health visitor or your GP. The telephone number of your health authority will be in the phone book.

FPA (Family Planning Association) provides guidance and information on contraception and sexual health. A low cost national telephone helpline, tel. 0845 310 1334 is open Monday - Friday 09.00am - 07.00pm, website address **www.fpa.org.uk**

The National Childbirth Trust provides information and support in pregnancy, childbirth, and early parenthood. Website address, **www.nctpregnancyandbabycare.com**

EDUCATION
Going to school

Education in Britain is free and compulsory for all children between the ages of 5-16. It is a parent or guardian's responsibility to make sure that their child goes to school, arrives on time, and attends for the whole session. Failure to do this can result in the parent or guardian being prosecuted. Details of local schools are available from the local education authority office. The office address and telephone number are in the phone book.

Children's education in Britain is normally divided into two separate stages. They begin primary education at the age of five and this usually lasts until they are eleven. Then they move to secondary school, where they stay until they reach sixteen, seventeen, or eighteen years of age.

Some areas of the country also offer free nursery education, which children can attend from the age of three.

Primary schools

These are almost always mixed sex, and usually located close to a child's home. Children tend to be with the same group throughout the day, and one teacher has responsibility for most of the work that they do.

Parents are strongly encouraged to help their children, particularly with reading and writing, and small amounts of homework are set to all children, even during the early years at school.

Most parents arrange for their children to be accompanied to school by a responsible adult if they are not able to take them there themselves.

Secondary schools

Most children transfer at the age of 11 – usually to their nearest secondary school, though the law allows parents in England and Wales to express preferences for other schools too. A place has to be offered at the parents' preferred school unless the school has more applicants than places; in that case it will admit the children who have highest priority under its published admission arrangements which can vary a little in different areas.

Most secondary schools cater for both sexes. They tend to be much larger than primary schools. Information on schools in your area, whether they tend to have more applicants than places, which applicants get priority if schools are over-subscribed, and how to apply for a secondary school place, is available from your local education authority office – which can also tell you whether, if your child attended a particular school, you would have to pay any costs of getting the child there and back.

Costs

State education in Britain is free. Parents are expected to make sure that their child has a pen, pencil, ruler etc. but the cost of other more specialised equipment, books, examination fees and the cost of visits undertaken during school hours that are part of the National Curriculum or an examination syllabus should all be covered by the school.

Parents are, however, expected to pay for their child's school uniform and items of sports wear. Charges may also be made for music lessons and for board and lodging on residential trips. Schools may ask parents for voluntary contributions for school time activities - but no pupil may be left out of an activity if their parents or guardian cannot or do not contribute.

However, parents on a low income are entitled to receive help with these costs, and with the cost of school lunches, which are provided each day in all schools. The Citizens Advice Bureau or the local education authority office will be able to tell you if you are entitled to help with the costs of your child's education.

Church and other faith schools

The historical development of education in England and Wales has meant that a number of primary and secondary schools have a strong connection with either the Anglican or Roman Catholic Churches. In some parts of the country there are a small number of state schools linked to other faiths. More information on how to get your child a place at a particular school, including a faith school, is available from your local education authority office.

Independent schools

There are about 2,500 independent schools in Britain, catering for about eight per cent of the school population. They are privately organised and are neither run nor financed by the state. They vary greatly in size, but are generally smaller than comparable state schools. In almost every case, parents are expected to pay the full cost of tuition and associated costs, such as boarding fees. All must be officially registered and are open to inspection in the same way as state schools. They are not required to cover the same curriculum as state schools, but many do.

The language used to describe these schools can be confusing. They are usually termed "public schools", even though they are privately run.

The school curriculum

All state primary and secondary schools in England must follow the National Curriculum. This covers English, maths, science, design and technology, information and communication technology (ICT), history, geography, modern foreign languages, art and design, music, physical education (PE) and citizenship.

Schools must, by law, also provide religious education (RE) to all pupils, although parents can choose to withdraw their children from these lessons. Religious education as taught in schools reflects the British Christian religious tradition, but also takes into account the other principal religions represented in Britain.

Help with English

If your child's main language is not English, the school may be able to make arrangements for extra language support from a specialist teacher and suggest ways in which you might be able to provide further support out of school or in the home.

Careers education

All children at school receive careers advice from the age of 14 upwards, and schools should be able to help students and their parents with questions about entry requirements for particular careers.

Connexions is a national service, with offices throughout the country, able to give information and practical help about career options. The address and contact details of your local office are available from the Connexions website **www.connexions-direct.com** or tel 080 800 13219.

Parents and schools

Parents and guardians are usually asked to inform the school on the first day that their child is away from school, and to send a letter explaining the reason for the absence with the child on their return.

All schools now ask parents to sign a home-school agreement. This is a list of things that both the school and the parent or guardians agree to do to make sure that pupils are educated as well as possible.

Each year parents receive a written report on their child's progress in school, followed by an opportunity for parents to discuss this with teaching staff. Parents are always encouraged to get in touch with the school if they have any concerns about their child.

Many schools, particularly primary schools, receive a great deal of practical support from parents. Parents go into school to listen to children read, provide extra supervision for art, swimming, and games lessons, and also help to raise extra money for the school, through the school or parent-teacher association.

A number of places on a school's governing body are automatically reserved for parents. Parent governors are elected to the governing body in an election open only to parents. Each year the school's governing body produces an Annual Report for parents. Governing bodies will hold an annual parents evening each year, but will only do so if more than 15 parents indicate that they wish to attend such a meeting.

Further education

After leaving school, many young people attend their local college either to improve their examination grades or to obtain new qualifications for their chosen career. Sometimes the courses are full-time, but most people usually work and study at the same time. Most courses are free of charge for students up to the age of 19, although students often have to pay for the cost of examination entries themselves.

Learning English

There are many courses available for people who wish to improve their skills in speaking, reading, writing, and understanding English. Courses are generally available at all levels. They are usually known as ESOL courses - English for Speakers of Other Languages - and are normally held in community and training centres or Further Education (FE) colleges.

Some courses help with basic English, others provide more advanced training, and may be linked to particular professions. Some courses are for women only. Demand for courses can vary in some areas so there may be a waiting list.

Many courses are free, or cost very little. For details contact your local library or college of further education. Online support for basic skills for adults in reading, writing, and maths is available from Skillswise, part of the BBC website, **www.bbc.co.uk/skillswise**

Much of the information contained in this book can be used in ESOL classes. Good English language skills are an important route to improving employment prospects.

Universities

An increasing number of young people in Britain now go to university. Many take a year out after leaving school (known as a gap year) to earn money, to travel and to broaden their experience.

Applications for university are normally made by mid January for enrolment the following September but applications can be made later. Schools and colleges will help their students with this process.

Most students today who attend English or Welsh universities are required to make a contribution *towards* the cost of their tuition fees and to pay for their living expenses. In Scotland the system is different and there are no tuition fees.

At the moment the maximum that a full-time student would be asked to pay towards their tuition fees would be £1,125 each year. How much a student could be asked to pay depends on their income and the income of their family. Currently, the Government pays for all the fees for around 40 percent of full-time students. Subject to Parliamentary approval, the Government is planning to make changes to the funding system for full-time students from September 2006. From that date universities would be able to charge tuition fees up to a maximum of £3,000, but unlike now students would not have to pay anything before or during their studies towards their fees. Instead they would combine their loan for fees with their loan for living costs which they would not have to start repaying until after they have left university and their earnings are over a certain level.

Most students at university take out a student loan through a government backed scheme to help with living costs. These are offered at a very low rate of interest. Students pay back this loan after they have left university and when their earnings reach a certain level. The money is automatically deducted from their salary, in the same way as tax or national insurance.

LEISURE
What's on?

Details of plays, films, music, exhibitions, and other special events are advertised in local newspapers. Your local library and tourist information centre will also have special notice boards and display stands advertising local events. Many public museums and galleries open free of charge.

Film, video and DVD

Most large towns and cities in Britain have a modern cinema complex showing several different films at the same time. A classification system indicates the suitability of films (and video and DVD) for children. Children below the specified age should not be admitted to films, nor should they be allowed to buy or hire videos.

All films receive one of the following classifications

U (universal)	Suitable for anyone aged four years or over
PG (parental guidance)	Suitable for general viewing, but some scenes may not be suitable for children without guidance from parents
12	No one under 12 admitted, unless with an adult
15	No one under 15 admitted
18	No one under 18 admitted

Videos and DVDs are widely available to rent. Most stores operate a simple membership system, requiring proof of name and address. Parents may well think that some videos, like some late night television broadcasts, are unsuitable for children.

Sport, clubs and societies

Councils and large libraries keep a record of local clubs and societies, with information on what they do, when they meet, and whom to contact to join. In the same way, the local leisure centre will have details of all the sports clubs who use the centre. Both libraries and leisure centres often organise extra activities for children and families during the school holidays.

General information on what is available in your area is listed on the local council website.

Sites of interest

A very good way of discovering places and sites of interest in the countryside is to make use of the large network of public footpaths, which give access to some of the most beautiful countryside in Britain.

On the ground, paths are usually - but not always - marked with signposts. But, for an accurate guide, you will need to look at a large scale Ordnance Survey Map of an area, preferably 1:25,000. These are sold in bookshops and tourist information centres, but can also be borrowed free of charge from libraries.

Access to many areas of countryside in Britain is kept open by the work of the National Trust. This is a large charitable organisation that seeks to preserve and protect important buildings and landscapes in Britain. Details of properties and areas open to the public can be found on the National Trust website, **www.nationaltrust.org.uk**

Adult education

A lot of people in Britain join a class to improve their general education, to learn a new hobby, or to improve their employment skills. There is usually a wide choice available, covering all kinds of activities. These might include sports like badminton or karate, arts and crafts, music, dancing, plus practical and academic courses, such as car maintenance or a foreign language. Costs are relatively low, and classes take place during the day or early evening. Courses usually begin in September. Details of these are available from June onwards at your local public library and adult education centre.

Television and radio

There is a wide choice of television and radio programmes available to people living in almost every part of Britain.

Everyone in Britain with a television, video recorder, or a computer that is capable of receiving broadcast television programmes must, by law, have a television licence. One licence covers all the equipment in a single home. If rooms are rented separately, a licence must be obtained for the TV equipment in each room.

A colour television licence costs £121 (2004) and lasts for 12 months. Licences for black-and-white televisions only are much cheaper. Free television licences are available for anyone aged 75 years or over.

A television licence is available from any post office or, by post, from Customer Services, TV Licensing, Bristol BS98 1TL. For customer enquiries, tel 0870 576 3763. It may be paid for in one lump sum, by instalments, or with TV licence stamps, available from post offices. Further details are available from the Citizens Advice Bureau and TV Licensing.

Vans with detection equipment tour the streets from time to time to identify signals from houses or flats whose residents have not bought a licence. Fines for failing to have a television licence can be heavy.

Money raised from the licence fee is used to pay for BBC radio and television programmes. The cost of other radio and television programmes broadcast in Britain is largely paid for through advertising and subscription.

Pubs

Public houses or pubs, as they are known, are an important part of local life in many parts of Britain. Groups of friends normally buy "rounds" of drinks, where the person whose turn it is will buy drinks for all the members of the group. It is sometimes difficult to get served when pubs are busy: people do not queue, but the bar staff will usually try and serve those who have been waiting longest at the bar first. If you spill a stranger's drink by accident, it is good manners (and prudent) to offer to buy another.

It is an offence to sell alcohol in a bar, pub, off-licence, or supermarket to anyone below the age of 18. It is also an offence for someone under 18 to buy, or to try to buy, alcohol. Young people are, with the landlord's agreement, able to go into a pub from the age of 14, but they must not drink alcohol. From the age of 16, however, they may buy and drink wine, beer, cider or perry with a meal in a hotel, restaurant, or in part of a pub that is set aside to sell meals.

A number of towns and cities in Britain now ban the consumption of alcohol in public, making it an offence to drink alcohol in the street or in a public park. There is a social problem now with some groups of young people who deliberately drink too much (called "binge" drinking) and can then become noisy and aggressive on the streets. The government and the most of the owners of pubs and bars are trying to tackle this problem.

Betting and gambling

Young people under the age of 18 are not allowed into betting shops or gaming clubs. No one under 16 may buy a lottery ticket or scratch card, nor can they collect any winnings on behalf of someone else.

Pets

Britain is famous for being a nation of animal lovers, and many people in Britain keep pets. Just under half the households in the UK own a pet. Dogs and cats are the most popular animals.

Strict laws require owners to care for their animals and to make sure that they do not suffer unnecessarily. These laws apply to all pets - large or small. Pet owners are also responsible for any damage that their animal causes if they knew (or should have known) that it was likely to cause such damage. A national charity called the RSPCA (Royal Society for the Prevention of Cruelty to Animals) employs many inspectors to prosecute cruel owners but also to care for abandoned animals.

All dogs in a public place must be kept under control. Dog owners are also responsible for making sure that their dog does not foul a footpath. The person in charge of the dog commits an offence if they fail to clear up after the animal.

Vaccinations and treatment for animals is available from veterinary surgeons, known as vets. Fees can be high. It is a good idea to check first how much the treatment will cost. A charity called the PDSA (People's Dispensary for Sick Animals) provides free veterinary care for people receiving housing or council tax benefit who live within the area of one of their pet hospitals or practices. Further information is available form their website, **www.pdsa.org.uk**

Holidays and traditions

Most working people aged 16 and over are entitled to at least four weeks' paid holiday per year. Holidays from work usually need to be booked in advance and with the employer's agreement.

Public holidays

Britain has relatively few public holidays compared with other European states. They are usually described as Bank Holidays because they are days when banks are officially closed.

Although schools and most places of employment close on bank holidays, many shops remain open and most essential services are available.

In a few parts of the country there are still some traditional times when holidays are taken, and public buildings may be closed.

Public holidays in England, Wales, Scotland and Northern Ireland

January 1st	New Year's Day
January 2nd	Scotland only
March 17th	St Patrick's Day (Northern Ireland only)
March/April	Good Friday: two days before Easter Sunday
March/April	Easter Monday: the day after Easter Sunday
May	May Bank Holiday: the first Monday in May
May	Spring Bank Holiday: the last Monday in May
August	August Bank Holiday: the first Monday in August (Scotland only)
August	August Bank Holiday: the last Monday in August (England, Wales & N Ireland only)
December 25th	Christmas Day
December 26th	Boxing Day

The date on which Easter Sunday falls varies each year, but is always in March or April. More details of religious and traditional festivals in the UK are given on pp.43-44.

TRAVEL AND TRANSPORT
Trains, coaches, buses

The National Rail Enquiry Service provides details of train service, times, and fares tel 08457 48 49 50, also available from the **website, www.nationalrail.co.uk** For local bus times, tel 0870 608 2 608, or use the Traveline website, **www.traveline.org.uk** Information on long distance coach travel is available from National Express, **www.nationalexpress.com** or tel 08705 80 80 80.

As a general rule, tickets on trains and the London Underground should be bought before travel. Passengers who travel on trains or the London Underground without a ticket may be charged an on-the-spot penalty and the full cost of their fare.

The cost of train travel normally depends on the day and time you wish to travel. Travelling outside the times most people travel to and from work is always cheaper as well as more comfortable. When buying a ticket, always state when you plan to travel.

Discount tickets are available for families, people aged 60 and over, disabled people and students and young people under 26. Details are available from your local station and **www.nationalrail.co.uk**

Taxis

All taxis and minicabs should be licensed and display a licence plate. Unlicensed cabs are illegal. They are not insured to carry fare-paying passengers, which means that if there is an accident, passengers have few rights to compensation.

Driving

Drivers in Britain must be 17 years of age to drive a car or motorcycle, 18 years of age to drive a medium sized lorry and 21 years old to drive a large lorry or bus. Special licences are generally required to drive medium and large lorries, minibuses and buses with more than eight passenger seats.

The driving licence

Anyone who drives a motor vehicle on a public road must have a driving licence. It is an offence to drive without a licence. A full driving licence is obtained by passing the driving test. Drivers may continue to use their licence until they are 70. Licences for drivers over 70 are issued for three years at a time.

A full driving licence is obtained in three stages:

❶ *Apply for a provisional licence.* With this you can drive a motorcycle, up to 125cc, or car. The vehicle must be taxed and insured and must display "L" for learner plates, or "D" plates in Wales. Learner drivers must not drive on a motorway and, if they are driving a car, they must have someone with them in the front passenger seat who is over 21 and has had a full driving licence for at least three years. This person must be fit to drive and must not have more than the legally permitted amount of alcohol in their blood. Application forms for a provisional licence can be obtained from any post office.

❷ *Pass a written theory test.* This takes about 40 minutes to complete.

❸ *Pass a practical test.* This test also takes about 40 minutes to complete and requires drivers to demonstrate their skills in a range of traffic conditions. There are driving test centres in all large towns and cities.

Overseas licences

A person who comes to Britain from overseas, and drives on UK roads, must be able to produce a valid driving licence. Anyone who drives a motor vehicle on the road, and is unable to produce a valid driving licence, commits an offence. A full driving licence obtained from a country within the European Union, or from Iceland, Liechtenstein, or Norway, may be used in Britain for as long as the licence remains valid.

If your driving licence is from any other country, you may drive any category of small vehicle shown on your licence for up to 12 months. However, during this period you must obtain a provisional British licence and pass both your theory and practical driving tests. If you do not, you will not have a full licence to drive on British roads.

Motor insurance

It is an offence to drive, ride, or even place a motor vehicle on the road without proper insurance. The penalties for this are very heavy, and it makes no difference to say it was a mistake. Drivers without insurance face heavy fines and possible disqualification from driving. It is also an offence for someone to allow their car or motorcycle to be used by a person not insured to drive it.

Road tax and MOT

Any motor vehicle that is being used, or is standing, on a public road must display an up-to-date road tax disc, available from a post office. Vehicles that are not properly taxed may be clamped or towed away. A penalty is charged to recover the car, plus the cost of the road tax.

Each year, vehicles that are three or more years old must be taken for a Ministry of Transport (MOT) test. This is carried out at any approved garage. Failure to have an MOT certificate is a criminal offence, and invalidates a driver's insurance.

Safety

Seat belts (front and rear) must be worn by drivers and passengers. Motorcyclists and their passenger must both wear crash helmets. However this regulation does not apply to a follower of the Sikh faith, while wearing a turban. It is also an offence to drive whilst holding a mobile phone.

Speed limits Cars and motorcycles are limited to:

30 mph	in built-up areas, unless otherwise shown
60 mph	on single carriageways
70 mph	on motorways and dual carriageways.
	Speed limits are lower for buses, lorries, and cars towing caravans

Police officers can check, or breathalyse any driver they believe has more than the permitted amount of alcohol in their body. The driver will be arrested if the test is positive or they refuse to take the test. Driving under the influence of alcohol is seen as a very serious crime. Disqualification from driving is almost automatic.

Accidents If you are involved in a motoring accident…

- Don't drive away without stopping. It's a criminal offence.
- If someone is injured, ring for the police and ambulance service (dial 999 or 112).
- Get the names, addresses, vehicle registration numbers, and insurance details of the other drivers involved.
- Give your details to anyone who has a reasonable need to know them - such as the other driver or passengers, or a police officer attending the accident.
- Make a detailed note of everything that happened and contact your insurance company as soon as possible.
- If you admit that the accident was your fault, you may find that your insurance company will refuse to pay up on your insurance policy. It is better, therefore, to remain quiet and allow the insurance company to sort the matter out.

IDENTITY DOCUMENTS

At present there is no requirement for UK citizens to carry identity cards. However, in 2003, the Government stated that, over the next ten years, it intended to begin the process of building a base for a national compulsory identity card scheme.

Proving your identity

There are a number of occasions in everyday life when you may be asked to prove your identity. These might include opening a bank account (see p. 85), renting accommodation, signing up for a college course, joining a library, or hiring a car.

Different organisations may ask for different documents as proof of identity (ID). Often they require a signature, photograph, or proof of current address. It is helpful to have several different kinds of documents available. These could include:

- official documents from the Home Office confirming your immigration status,
- Certificate of Identity,
- passport or Travel Document,
- National Insurance Number Card,
- provisional or full driving licence,
- copy of a recent gas, electricity, or telephone bill containing your name and current address,
- a rent, or benefits book.
  When boarding a commercial aircraft you may need a photo ID or a passport.

References

You may, on occasions, also be asked to provide the name of a referee. This is someone who knows you well and can comment on your character or capabilities and can confirm the information that you have given about yourself. You may be asked to provide one or more references when you are applying for a bank account, for work, or for a driving licence.

A referee is usually someone who has lived in this country for a number of years and has a position of responsibility in the community. It could be a person with a professional qualification, such as a teacher or social worker, or a manager in a voluntary or community organisation. Family members are not usually accepted as referees.

6 Employment

LOOKING FOR WORK

If you are looking for work, or thinking about changing your job, there are a number of ways in which you can find out about work that is available.

However, anyone seeking work in the UK should check, before taking up employment, that their status allows them to do so. Employers are also required to make sure that anyone they employ is legally entitled to work in Britain. Guidance on this is available on the Home Office website, "Working in the UK" **www.workingintheuk.gov.uk**

Jobs in the area where you live are advertised in local newspapers, at the local Jobcentre, and in employment agencies. The address and telephone number of your nearest **Jobcentre Plus** is in the telephone book. Employment agencies are also listed in the Yellow Pages and Thomson Local guides.

Jobcentre Plus is run by the government Department for Work and Pensions. Trained staff are able to give advice and help about finding and applying for employment as well as assisting in gaining benefits. They also have access to interpreters.

The website **www.jobcentreplus.gov.uk** lists vacancies and gives general information on benefits and training opportunities.

A low cost telephone service, Jobseeker Direct, is also available, with details of local job vacancies, tel 0845 60 60 234. Lines are open weekdays, 09.00am - 06.00pm, and 09.00am - 01.00pm, Saturdays.

Sometimes jobs are advertised on supermarket boards and in shop windows, but these are often part-time, and not usually well paid.

If you want to work for a particular company or organisation, you will normally find vacancies advertised on their website.

National newspapers also carry advertisements for jobs. These are usually for work requiring special training or qualifications, based in major cities.

Qualifications

If you have qualifications that were obtained in another country, you can check how they compare to similar British qualifications at the National Academic Recognition Information Centre for the UK, **www.naric.org.uk**

For information contact UK NARIC, ECCTIS Ltd, Oriel House, Oriel Road, Cheltenham, Gloucestershire GL50 1XP, tel 01242 260010, fax 01242 258611, email: **naric@ecctis.co.uk**

Applications

Interviews for lower paid work, or jobs advertised locally, can often be arranged by telephone or by enquiring in person. If you apply for a better-paid job, you are usually asked to write a letter of application and enclose a summary of your qualifications and past experience, known as a curriculum vitae or CV.

In the letter of application you normally state why you are applying for the job and why you believe you are suitable. Your CV gives details of your education, your qualifications, the work you have done in the past, and details of your skills and interests that are relevant to the post for which you are applying.

If possible, try to make sure that your letter of application and CV are typed, rather than handwritten. It will almost certainly improve your chances of being called for interview.

An employer will often ask for the names and addresses of one or two referees. These are people - such as a previous employer, or college tutor - who have known you in the past and are able to write a short report, or reference, on your suitability for work. The names of personal friends or family members are not normally acceptable as referees (see also p.107).

Interviews

It is important in an interview for employers and applicants to be truthful about the work. Employers should explain exactly what the job involves and give full details of pay, holidays, and conditions of work. If these are not clear, ask for more information. In fact asking questions and showing interest in the work usually improves your chance of being offered the job.

Whilst everyone looking for work wants to present themselves as favourably as possible, it is important to be honest about qualifications or experience. If a person is offered a job and it is later discovered that the information they gave at interview or on their application form was wrong or misleading, they are likely to be immediately dismissed.

Criminal record

If you are successful in interview, particularly if the job involves working with children or other vulnerable people, you may be asked to allow a check to be made on your criminal record. For further information contact the Criminal Records Bureau (CRB), an agency of the Home Office, CRB Infoline, tel 0870 90 90 811.

Training

There are many opportunities for people to improve their qualifications for work. Training may be available through work, home study, or a college course. Your local library and college will have details of courses in the area in which you live. Websites such as **www.worktrain.gov.uk** and **www.learndirect.co.uk** enable you to research in some detail training and courses that are available.

Learndirect is an organisation with a network of online training courses developing employment skills and life long learning, with over 2,000 local centres throughout the country. Charges are made for courses, but many offer free starter or taster sessions. A free information and advice line is available, tel 0800 100 900.

Volunteering and work experience

Sometimes people find work by offering themselves as volunteers. This can be a good way of showing others the kind of work that they can do, and may lead to a paid job. Not all jobs provide opportunities for volunteering, but many people find that it is a very satisfying activity, and can be a good way of becoming more involved in the local community.

Your local library can help you find details of who to contact for volunteering opportunities in your area. There are also many Websites with information and advice on volunteering, for example **www.do-it.org.uk**, **www.worktrain.gov.uk**, **www.volunteering.org.uk**, and **www.justdosomething.net**

Childcare

It is Government policy to help people find employment by improving the provision of childcare. Some employers are able to help with this. For information about the different types of childcare and childminders available in your area, and details of registered childminders, see the ChildcareLink website, **www.childcarelink.gov.uk**, or tel 08000 96 02 96.

EQUAL RIGHTS AND DISCRIMINATION

It is against the law in England and Wales for employers to discriminate against someone at work because of their

- sex
- nationality, race, colour, or ethnic group
- disability
- religion, or
- sexual orientation.

This means that a person should not be refused work, training, or promotion because of their sex, the colour of their skin, their country of origin, their sexuality, religion or because of a disability. The law also says that men and women, who do the same job at work, or work of equal value, should receive equal pay.

At the moment it is not against the law to discriminate against someone because of their age, although this is likely to change by 2006.

There are a small number of jobs where the discrimination laws do not apply. Discrimination is not against the law, for example, when the job involves working for someone in their own house.

Almost all the laws protecting people at work apply whether you are in a full or part-time job. You can get more information about the law protecting people from race discrimination from the **Commission for Racial Equality**. The **Equal Opportunities Commission** can help with questions of sex discrimination, and the **Disability Rights Commission** deals with disability matters.

Each organisation provides advice and information and can, in certain circumstances, take up cases on behalf of individuals and undertake general investigations.

The Commission for Racial Equality, St Dunstan's House, 201-211 Borough High Street, London SE1 1GZ, tel 020 7939 0000, fax 020 7939 0001, **www.cre.gov.uk**

The Disability Rights Commission DRC Helpline, FREEPOST MID02164 Stratford upon Avon, CV37 9BR, tel 08457 622 633, fax 08457 778 878, **www.drc.org.uk**

The Equal Opportunities Commission, Arndale House, Arndale Centre, Manchester M4 3EQ, tel 0845 601 5901, fax 0161 838 1733, **www.eoc.org.uk**

Sexual harassment

Indecent remarks, inappropriate touching, or comments about your sex life are all examples of sexual harassment. Unwanted or offensive behaviour of this kind is against the law.

If – as a woman, or a man – you suffer this kind of behaviour at work, you are advised to tell a trusted friend or colleague and to ask the harasser to stop. If the problem continues, report the person to your employer or trade union. Employers should treat complaints of this kind very seriously and take effective action to deal with it. If you are not satisfied with your employer's response, you can seek further help from the Equal Opportunities Commission, your trade union, or the Citizens Advice Bureau.

Working in Europe

British citizens can work in any country that is a member of the European Union. Generally speaking, they have exactly the same employment rights as citizens of that state.

AT WORK
A written statement

Within two months of starting work, your employer should give you a written statement setting out all the details and conditions of your work. This should show details of your pay, hours, holidays, sick pay, pension. It should also state the period of notice that you and your employer must give if either of you wish the employment to end.

The statement is an important piece of paper and is very useful to both sides if there is ever a disagreement over the work you are required to do.

Both employers and employees have legal responsibilities at work. Employers should pay employees for the work that they do, they should treat them fairly and should take reasonable care for their health and safety. Employees should carry out their duties with reasonable skill and care, to obey all reasonable instructions and not to damage their employer's business.

Pay, hours and holidays

Your pay is something that is agreed between you and your employer. However, there is a minimum wage in Britain, which everybody aged 18 or over should receive. The minimum rate of pay (from October 2005) for someone aged 16-17 is £3.00 per hour; aged 18-21 is £4.25 per hour, and is £5.05 for someone aged 22 and over. Employers who pay their workers less than this are breaking the law.

Your statement will show the number of hours that you are expected to work. Sometimes you might be asked to work longer than this. It is up to you whether you do so, but your employer should not put unreasonable pressure on you to work longer than you have agreed.

If you are ever absent from work it is important to give your employer as much warning as possible.

Most people who are working and aged 16 or over are entitled to at least four weeks' paid holiday per year, including time off for national holidays (see p. 53 & p. 103).

Your employer must give you a pay slip, or similar written statement, each time you are paid, showing your exact pay and how much money is being taken off for tax and national insurance.

Tax

Unless you are self-employed (see p. 118), tax is automatically taken from your earnings by your employer and paid directly to the HM Revenue and Customs, the government department responsible for collecting taxes. Money raised from income tax pays for services provided by the government, such as roads, education, police, and the armed forces.

The HM Revenue and Customs may ask you, on occasions, to fill in a tax return giving full details of your financial position. It is important to complete and return this form as soon as possible. Help is available from the Inland Revenue self-assessment helpline, tel 0845 300 45 55.

National Insurance

Almost everybody in Britain who is in paid work (and this includes the self-employed) must pay National Insurance (NI) contributions. Money raised is used to help pay for the Health Service and the state retirement pension. Employees automatically have the money deducted from their earnings each week or month. Those who are self-employed usually pay NI contributions every three months.

Anyone who fails to pay enough NI contributions will not be able to receive certain benefits and will not qualify for a full state retirement pension.

Getting a National Insurance number

Just before their sixteenth birthday, all young people in Britain are sent a National Insurance number that is used to identify their National Insurance contribution record. Most newly accepted refugees are now given a number automatically. If you don't already have a National Insurance number, you will almost certainly need one when you start work. Almost all employers require this.

You can apply for a National Insurance number at your local social security or Jobcentre Plus office. You will need to show your birth certificate, passport, and the documents given to you by the Home Office allowing you to stay in this country. It is a good idea to telephone the social security or Jobcentre Plus office beforehand to make an appointment and to check exactly what items to bring.

Pensions

Everyone in Britain who has paid enough national insurance contributions is entitled to receive a pension from the state when they reach state retirement age.

The state retirement age for men is 65 years of age, and for women it is 60. However, women's retirement age will gradually be increased to 65 between 2010 and 2020. Full details of the state pension scheme is given on the Pension Service website, **www.thepensionservice.gov.uk**

An increasing number of people in Britain also receive a pension through their work, and many also contribute to a personal pension as well.

Getting good advice about pensions is very important. Talking to an independent financial adviser is a good start. Local financial advisers are listed in the Yellow Pages or can be found online at **www.unbiased.co.uk**

The Pensions Advisory Service gives free and confidential advice on occupational and personal pensions. Their helpline telephone number is 0845 601 2923, and their website address **www.opas.org.uk**

Health and safety

Employers have a legal duty to make sure that they provide safe arrangements for work for their employees. There is also a legal duty on workers to obey safety regulations and to work safely and responsibly.

If you are worried about health and safety, raise the matter with your supervisor. Your employer may not dismiss you or treat you unfairly for raising genuine concerns, as long as you follow the right procedures.

Trade unions

Trade unions in Britain are organisations that try to improve the pay and working conditions of their members. They also give their members advice over problems at work and will act on their behalf over difficulties with their employer.

It is your choice as to whether you join a trade union or not. You cannot be forced to join, but if you do, your employer may not dismiss you for doing so.

Details of trade unions in Britain, and the benefits membership may provide, are available from the Trades Union Congress (TUC) website, **www.tuc.org.uk**, which also contains useful summaries of rights at work.

Problems at work

If you are experiencing difficulties at work of any kind, it is a good idea to speak to your supervisor, or someone else in a position of responsibility, as soon as possible. If you belong to a trade union, your union representative may also be able to help.

It is almost always helpful to get advice before taking any action. Your local Citizens Advice Bureau or Law Centre are good places to visit first. ACAS (the Advisory, Conciliation and Arbitration Service) run a national helpline, offering information and advice on your rights at work, tel 08457 47 47 47.

Losing your job

Employees who seriously misbehave at work are likely to be dismissed immediately. Anyone who fails to do their job properly, or is unacceptably late or absent from work, is entitled to be given a warning. If their conduct doesn't improve, they will probably be given notice to leave. If you find yourself in this position, your trade union, a solicitor, a Law Centre or the Citizens Advice Bureau can explain your legal rights and tell you if you have been treated fairly.

Unfair dismissal

If you are dismissed from work unfairly, or life at work is made so difficult that you feel you have to leave, you may be entitled to compensation. Employers who behave in this way are breaking the law.

If this happens to you, you can take your case to an employment tribunal, which is a court specialising in employment matters. If you are successful, you may receive compensation for the losses you have suffered as a result of losing your job.

You'll need advice on whether you have a good case – and if you do, on what is the best action to take. A solicitor will be able to help you with this. A good starting point is to discuss the matter with your trade union, the Citizens Advice Bureau or a Law Centre, but don't delay. After your dismissal, you normally have only three months in which to make a complaint.

Redundancy

If you lose your job because the company you work for no longer needs someone to do your job or cannot afford to continue to employ you, you may be entitled to redundancy pay. The amount will depend on the length of time you have been employed. Again your trade union, the Citizens Advice Bureau, a Law Centre, or a solicitor will be able to advise you.

Unemployment

If you become unemployed you will be entitled to claim a benefit called Jobseeker's Allowance. This is for men and women, aged 16-65, who are unemployed and actively looking for work.

Your local Jobcentre Plus office will help you with your claim. Further advice is available from the Citizens Advice Bureau and the Jobcentre Plus website, **www.jobcentreplus.gov.uk**

New Deal

People who have been unemployed and claiming Jobseeker's Allowance for six months or more are usually required to join the New Deal programme if they wish to continue to receive benefit. New Deal gives people help and advice on finding work and checks on their progress. There are different schemes for young and older people.

The government also runs programmes of work-based learning for young people and adults, giving training to people whilst they work. A wage or an allowance is paid, with the opportunity to attend college for a day a week to gain a new qualification.

Information on all the above schemes, together with any others available in your area, are obtainable from Jobcentre Plus, **www.jobcentreplus.gov.uk**, or your local Citizens Advice Bureau.

EXPECTING A BABY
For mothers

If you are expecting a baby, you have a legal right to time off work for antenatal care and to at least 18 weeks' maternity leave. These rights are available to both full and part-time workers, and it makes no difference how long you have worked for your employer. However, it is important to follow the correct procedures in applying for maternity leave, otherwise you run the risk of losing your job.

You may also be entitled to maternity pay - but this depends on how long you have been working for your employer. The personnel officer at work, your trade union representative, or the local Citizens Advice Bureau can help you with all these matters.

For fathers

Fathers who have worked for their employer for at least 41 weeks are entitled to up to two weeks' time off from work, with pay, when their child is born. The rate of pay may not be as high as you normally receive, and again it is important to inform your employer well in advance.

Further information on rights for mothers and fathers who are expecting a child is available from Maternity Alliance, an independent charity working to improve the rights and services for all pregnant mothers, new mothers and their families. The telephone number of their information line is 020 7490 7638, and their website address, **www.maternityalliance.org.uk**

WORKING FOR YOURSELF
Tax

If you set up business on your own and become *self-employed*, you must keep detailed records of what you earn and spend on the business.

This is because self-employed people are responsible for paying their own tax and national insurance, and each year must submit their business accounts to the Inland Revenue. It is almost essential to consult an accountant to help you make sure that you pay the correct tax and claim all the tax allowances to which you are entitled. The tax enforcement system is both efficient and strict, and the penalties for evasion are high.

As soon as you become self-employed, you should contact your local tax office (the telephone number is in the phone book) who will gladly answer questions and register you in the correct way for tax and National Insurance. There is an Inland Revenue helpline for the newly self-employed, tel 0845 915 4515.

Help and advice

Banks provide advice and free leaflets on setting up and running a business, and are also able to provide start-up loans. Government grants and other financial assistance may also be available. Details of these and advice on becoming self-employed and starting up a business are available from Business Link who have offices throughout the UK. For further information, tel 0845 600 9 006, or visit their website, **www.businesslink.gov.uk**

CHILDREN AT WORK

Children's work in Britain is strictly controlled by law, to protect them from exploitation and not to hinder their education. Although rules vary from one part of the country to another, children under the age of 14 are generally not allowed to work at all, except for occasional light farm work supervised by a parent.

Hours and time

By law, children aged 14 -16 may only do light work. Jobs that they are not allowed to do include milk delivery; the sale of alcohol, cigarettes, or medicines; work in a kitchen or chip shop; the use of dangerous machinery; or work that may cause them any kind of injury. Children who work are also required to have a medical certificate of fitness for work and an employment card issued by their local authority.

No child below the school leaving age of sixteen may work before 7am or after 7pm, and for more than one hour before the start of school. No child is allowed to work for more than 12 hours a week during term time, or for more than two hours on a school day, or on a Sunday. It makes no difference to these rules whether the child is working for a family business or another employer.

The local authority has a duty to check that the law is being obeyed. If it believes that a young person is working illegally, it can order that he or she is no longer employed. Employers who place children in any kind of danger can be heavily fined.

7 Sources of help and information

Throughout this guide there are details of where to get further information on a particular subject. This section tells you more about the general services offered by some of these advice centres and sources of information. Britain is rich in voluntary and community bodies, quite independent of the government, offering all kinds of help and advice

Be prepared

When you are looking for information or making an enquiry, there are a few things that you can do to improve your chances of success.

- Before you ask for information, think carefully about what you need to know. Sometimes it's helpful to write down a few key words that cover the main things that you want to say. You will also need a pen and paper to make a note of what you are told.

- Remember to have all the relevant documents with you. Sometimes you are asked for an account or reference number to help the person dealing with your case find your file.

- If possible avoid a long explanation. If you can, keep to the essential details.

- Make a note of the name of the person you are talking to. It may be useful to know this if you need to phone or call in again.

HELP FOR REFUGEES AND NEWCOMERS

There are many national and local organisations that offer information and advice for refugees and newcomers. Many specialise in helping asylum seekers. Your local Citizens Advice Bureau and library will be able to put you in touch with organisations in your area.

One of the largest of these organisations is the Refugee Council, covering England and Wales, which runs an enquiry desk open on Mondays, Wednesdays and Fridays, 10.00am-01.00pm, tel 0207 820 3085. Information is also available from their website **www.refugeecouncil.org.uk**

The Scottish Refugee Council offers information and advice to refugees and asylum seekers in Scotland, tel (free) 0800 085 6087. For further information also see their website, **www.scottishrefugeecouncil.org.uk**

PUBLIC LIBRARIES

Every town or city in Britain has a main public library, with smaller branch libraries located in the suburbs. In the past, public libraries were the main source of education for ambitious working people. A travelling library service is provided in most rural areas, usually calling in villages once a week. The address and telephone number of your local public library is listed under 'Libraries' in the phone book.

Most of the services offered by public libraries are free. They are paid for through local and national taxes. Anyone may use a library, but normally only members may borrow books and other items, such as CDs, audio or video tapes, and DVDs, or use the computer facilities. But it is easy to become a member by offering proof of local residence and identity.

Children

There is almost always a separate section in the library for children, and libraries are very keen to get them to join and form a reading habit.

Many libraries run special story time reading sessions during the week for very young children and their parents, along with reading and art activity sessions during school holidays for different age groups.

Books, CDs, audio and video tapes, and DVDs

All libraries have a collection of books for loan, which members can borrow for a specified period of time. Fines are imposed if books are returned after the date they are due back. Larger libraries also have CDs, audiotapes, videos, and DVDs for loan. These are loaned on a similar basis, for a small charge.

Reference

All libraries have a reference section, where books may be used, but not borrowed. Encyclopaedias, dictionaries, telephone directories, Yellow Pages and Thomson Local guides are all available in even the smallest libraries. Larger reference departments have newspapers too. They are useful if you are looking for a job or some special service.

Requests

If there are book or other items that you would like to borrow from the library but are already out on loan, you can ask for them to be reserved for you when they are returned. If the library does not have a copy of what you are looking for they may be able to obtain one from another library. This includes items in languages other than English, provided they are available in the UK.

Information

If you are looking for a particular piece of information, the library's reference department is normally the best place to start. One of the librarians at the desk will be able to help you with your enquiry. They can also tell you about local facilities and clubs, and if they don't have the information you require, they will probably be able to suggest where it might be obtained.

Language difficulties

Some libraries (and other council departments) subscribe to a telephone interpreting and translation service. This can link you, within a few minutes, to a speaker of one of thirty languages, who will translate the questions you would like to put to the librarian, and the answers that he or she gives.

Computers, photocopiers and fax machines

Almost all libraries - large and small - now have computers available for public use - for word processing and access to the Internet and e-mails. Access is free, but you usually need to book in advance. Use is normally restricted to library members. Photocopying and fax services are also available, for a charge, at many libraries.

Community links

Libraries are an excellent source of local and community information, with notice boards publicising meetings and local events, and a selection of free leaflets describing what is happening in the area. They may often have a meeting room available for hire.

CITIZENS ADVICE BUREAU (CAB)

The Citizens Advice Bureau service - normally called the CAB - gives free, impartial, and confidential advice. It is an independent organisation, with trained advisers, most of whom are volunteers. Millions of people use the service each year.

There are more than 2,000 CAB or Citizens Advice offices in towns and cities throughout Britain. You can find the address and telephone number of your nearest CAB from the phone book, your local library, or from the Citizens Advice Bureau's own website, **www.nacab.org.uk**

If you intend to visit a CAB, check the opening hours beforehand, as some offices are not open every day. Some CABs, however, are able to deal with enquiries by e-mail. See **www.nacab.org.uk** for details.

Practical help

CABs deal with enquiries across a wide range of topics. These include money matters, benefits and tax credits, pensions, employment, community care, the National Health Service, housing, immigration, domestic violence, and consumer problems.

As well as providing information, the CAB can also help with completing forms, writing letters, negotiating on behalf of clients, and representing them (or finding representation for them) at courts and tribunals. Like some libraries, they may also have access to interpreters.

There is also a CAB information website, **www.adviceguide.org.uk**, which gives up to date information on a wide range of topics in English, Welsh, Bengali, Chinese, Gujarati, Punjabi and Urdu.

The Citizens Advice Bureau welcomes volunteers. More information about this and how to get involved is available on the CAB website or from any CAB office.

THE POLICE SERVICE

Although police officers spend much of their time dealing with crime, they also have an important role in offering the public more general help and assistance.

In Britain it is quite usual to ask a police officer for directions in the street, or to seek advice at a police station. Police officers in the United Kingdom are protectors of the public, and are expected to be friendly and helpful to anyone who seeks their assistance.

Understandably, the police know most about matters to do with crime and community safety. If you are worried about your personal safety or have a more general question about the law relating to crime, you can telephone the police and ask for information at any time. In some parts of the country the police run a special telephone information line just for this purpose.

You can also ring the police to report a crime. For more information, see pp. 128-9.

The police can also help with other problems. They can often help, for example, when someone is locked out of their house or their car, or when they are worried about the safety of an elderly relative who is not answering the phone.

If you need help from the police, DO NOT dial 999 or 112, unless it is an emergency. For advice and non-urgent information telephone your local police station. The number is under 'Police' in the telephone book.

In an emergency, when there is a danger to life or a crime in progress, dial 999 for the police, fire, ambulance or coastguard service. You will be asked where you are calling from and the location of the accident or emergency. It saves a great deal of time if you can give this information quickly and clearly.

Do not dial 999 or 112 under any other circumstances. Calling out the emergency services unnecessarily - either deliberately or accidentally - is a punishable offence.

OTHER SOURCES OF INFORMATION
Yellow Pages

The yellow telephone directory (known as the Yellow Pages) gives contact details of all kinds of businesses and organisations in your local area. The main part of the directory lists the telephone numbers and addresses of a wide range of businesses and services (from Accident Claims to Zoos). At the front you will find details of local attractions, leisure and sport, together with useful numbers for information on transport and other local services.

Thomson Local

This is a local guide, which is delivered to some homes, and is always available in the library. It is full of local information, with maps of nearby town centres, details of local community organisations, businesses, helplines, travel, and entertainment.

Local authority services

Your local authority can provide information on all its services, such as education, social services, and public transport. Most of the services operated are listed in the business section of the phone book, under the name of the local authority.

Many local authorities produce general information guides on services in the area, and some have information and advice centres open five days a week. You can ask for the name and contact details of your local authority from the public library or the Citizens Advice Bureau.

Tourist information centres

There are tourist information centres throughout the country. As well as giving details of local tourist attractions, they are a good source of other local information, such as bus and train times, places of worship, doctors' surgeries etc.

Newspapers

National daily and Sunday newspapers, published in London, provide a wide range of news and sports coverage. Daily regional newspapers are available in many parts of the country, and all areas have local newspapers, usually published once a week. Newspapers in Britain are in private or corporate ownership and are independent of the state.

Free local newspapers are also delivered to many homes in Britain. These contain a large number of advertisements that are useful for finding second hand goods or household services - such as plumbers, electricians, or builders. They also give the late night opening times of chemists.

Television and radio

All the national radio and television stations give information on news and current events, with at least one nightly news broadcast on each channel.

There is also a network of local radio stations throughout the UK, providing music, news, and coverage of current and forthcoming events in the area, and often including minority community interests. The frequencies of local radio stations may be found in either newspapers or the *Radio Times*.

Televisions equipped to receive teletext provide up-to-the-minute information on news, weather, sport, finance, and travel.

The BBC website

The BBC website, **www.bbc.co.uk**, provides access to a huge range of local, national and international information, with a news service in more than 40 languages. If you need to find out more about a particular topic, it is often the best place to begin, with its major sections on education, science, history, business, and legal rights.

Post offices

There are post offices in towns and cities, and even small villages, throughout Britain. As well as taking mail and parcels for delivery, post offices also provide a number of other useful services.

All post offices have information about benefits and state pensions, and anyone who receives either of these can arrange for to collect them at a post office of their choice. Post offices also offer banking services and information about National Savings and Investments (Government-backed saving and investment services).

It is also possible to pay a whole range of bills at a post office. These include: telephone, cable TV, gas, electricity, water, TV licence, council tax, council rent, housing association rent, and Inland Revenue self assessment bills.

Post offices also provide application forms and information on motor vehicle and driving licences, television licences, and rod fishing licences.

Legal advice

For information on obtaining legal help and advice, see pp. 143-144.

Helplines

Many organisations, including government departments, run public telephone helplines, giving information and guidance on particular problems. Some of these numbers are listed in this guide.

If you would like to talk to someone about a particular subject, your local public library or Citizens Advice Bureau will be able to give you details of helplines. If you have access to a computer at home, a library or Internet café, a normal Internet search putting in the name of the subject (eg consumer rights or older people), followed by the words "helpline uk", will almost always reveal the names and contact details of an organisation able to provide information and advice.

Using the Internet

The usual way of finding information on the Internet is to type key word into a search engine, such as AltaVista, **www.altavista.com**, Google, **www.google.com** or Yahoo! **www.uk.yahoo.com**

If you put key words, such as *consumer rights*, into the search box, the search engine will look for the words *consumer* and *rights* quite separately and will probably produce several million results. To avoid this, type "*consumer rights*" in double inverted commas, and only websites with this combination of words will be listed.

Public access to computers is available through the local public library service (see p. 121) and Internet cafés, which offer Internet services for a small charge.

8 Knowing the law

THE RIGHTS AND DUTIES OF A CITIZEN
The police

The police in Britain are organised on a local basis, with each county or regional force responsible for the community that they serve. They are seen as a public service, giving protection to all.

The Home Secretary sets the general standards and priorities of the police force in Britain, but the work of the police in particular areas is determined by the local police force, of which there are 43 in England and Wales, eight in Scotland, and one in Northern Ireland.

Police officers in England and Wales do not usually carry firearms. Uniformed officers have a truncheon or baton to protect themselves against violence. Firearms are issued only to specially trained officers, and then only with the approval of a senior officer.

Reporting a crime

If you see a crime taking place, or are a victim of a crime, dial 999 or 112 in an EMERGENCY. The operator will ask you which service you require, why you need the police, and where they are required.

If the situation is NOT an emergency, contact your local police station either by phone, or in person. The telephone number will be under 'Police' in the phone book.

The police are there to be helpful, and you need have no fear at all of reporting a crime or asking them for help. If you suffer abuse or harassment from people, the police will take the matter very seriously. However if they are to help, you must tell them what has been happening and give them all the relevant facts.

Certain types of minor crime can now be reported online. See **www.online.police.uk** for details.

Police duties

The job of the police in Britain is to:

- protect life and property,
- prevent disturbances (known as keeping the peace), and
- prevent and detect crime.

Police officers must obey the law and also follow their own code of discipline. They must not misuse their authority, make a false statement, be rude or abusive, or commit racial discrimination. Police officers who are corrupt, or abuse their position, are severely punished.

Complaints

Anyone who believes that they have suffered or witnessed misconduct by the police may make an official complaint. Complaints may be made in person at any police station, in writing to the Chief Constable of the police force concerned, or to the Independent Police Complaints Commission. If it is a serious matter, it is a good idea to speak to a solicitor or to the Citizens Advice Bureau beforehand.

If the police ever stop you

When investigating a crime the police will often speak to members of the public to determine what has happened, who was involved etc. All citizens have a civic (rather than legal) duty to voluntarily help police officers to prevent crime and discover offenders. However, the police may stop a member of the public on foot in connection with a crime that has been committed, or one that they reasonably suspect may be about to take place. They may stop people in a vehicle at any time.

If you are stopped by the police, you should give the officer your name and address but, strictly speaking, you need not answer any further questions, though most law-abiding people wish to do so. However if you are obstructive or rude, or deliberately mislead the police, you may be at risk of being be arrested.

You are entitled to know the name of the officer who questioned you, the police station where he or she is based, and the reason why you have been stopped.

The police may ask you to come to the police station to answer further questions. It is up to you whether to attend. If you do go to a police station voluntarily, you are entitled to leave whenever you wish.

Search

The police can stop and search anyone whom they believe may be involved in committing certain offences, such as theft, burglary, possession of illegal drugs or possession of articles intended for committing criminal damage. They can also search the vehicle in which that person is travelling.

Police officers in England and Wales do not have the power to enter and search any building that they choose, but they may enter a property if they have a warrant (that is, special permission from a magistrate) to do so, or to arrest someone, to save life, and to prevent serious disturbance or damage.

Anyone being searched is entitled to know the name of the officer, the police station where they are based, and their reason for the search.

Arrest

If you are arrested and taken to a police station, a police officer will tell you the reason for your arrest. The officer will caution you saying that anything you say may be given as evidence later in court. You have the right to remain silent until you have seen a lawyer, see below.

If you have difficulty in understanding English, the police should provide an interpreter before interviewing you, unless the delay would result in serious harm to someone or serious damage to property.

A similar rule applies to the arrest of children or young people. The police should not normally interview a young person below the age of 17 without their parent or an 'appropriate adult' being present. An appropriate adult is someone such as a social worker, an adult friend, or teacher.

Information and advice

If you are arrested and detained at a police station, you will be given written details of three important legal rights:

❶ The right to see a solicitor.
❷ The right to have a message sent to a friend or member of your family, telling them where you are.
❸ The right to look at the codes of practice - guidelines that the police should follow when searching for and collecting evidence.

This written note also sets out the official police caution that is given to all police suspects. This states, '*You do not have to say anything. But it may harm your defence if you do not mention when questioned, something which you later rely on in court. Anything you do say may be given in evidence.*'

The caution means that the police cannot compel a person to answer questions. However, the failure of a suspect to answer questions at the police station (or in court) can form part of the evidence against them. The caution also states that anything a person does say to a police officer may be used as evidence in court.

The duty solicitor

In almost all circumstances, anyone who has been arrested or who goes to a police station voluntarily is entitled to legal advice, in private, from a duty solicitor, or a solicitor of their choice. A duty solicitor will work for a local firm, specialising in criminal law, and will have volunteered to provide the service on a rota basis. Typically this may be provided in person, but in some cases the advice will be provided over the telephone. The consultation with the duty solicitor is free.

If you have been arrested or are being questioned about a serious offence, or if you feel unsure about your legal position, you have the right not to answer questions (except to give your name and address) until you have a chance to speak to a solicitor.

The law

Every person in Britain has the right to equal treatment under the law. The law applies in the same way to everybody - regardless of who they are or where they are from.

Law may be divided into *criminal* and *civil* law. *Civil* law is a way of settling disputes between individuals or groups. *Criminal* law covers behaviour that is punishable by the state, such as assault or theft. These actions are crimes and are usually dealt with by the police, or some other authority - and not by the individuals concerned.

Victims of crime

Anyone who is a victim of a violent crime can apply to the Criminal Injuries Compensation Authority for compensation for their injuries. The crime must be reported to the police without delay, and the application for compensation must be made within two years of the incident that caused the injury. Details of the Criminal Injuries Compensation Authority are given on their website **www.cica.gov.uk**

Help and guidance to victims of crime is available from Victim Support. Their website address is **www.victimsupport.com** and their telephone number is in the local phone book. They also run a national helpline tel 0845 30 30 900.

It is important to be aware that in Britain it is an offence to carry a weapon, such as a gun, knife, or anything that is made or adapted to cause injury to someone, even if it is for self-defence.

Military service

Since 1960, there has been no requirement in Britain for either men or women to carry out compulsory military service.

HUMAN RIGHTS
The Human Rights Act

Britain has a long tradition of respect for basic human rights, and was one of the first countries to sign the European Convention on Human Rights. In 1998, the government passed the Human Rights Act, which incorporated nearly all these rights into law. These rights apply to everyone in the United Kingdom.

All laws in Britain must, as far as possible, follow the Human Rights Act 1998. British courts must follow the principles of the Convention, and public bodies, like the police, schools, and hospitals must carry out their work in a way that upholds the Human Rights Act.

More information on the Act is available from the Department of Constitutional Affairs, **www.dca.gov.uk**

The Human Rights Act lists 16 basic rights.

- The right to life: Everyone has the right to have their life protected by law. The State may take away someone's life in only very limited circumstances, for example when a police officer acts justifiably in self-defence.

- Prohibition of torture: No one should be tortured or punished in an inhuman or degrading way.

- Prohibition of slavery and forced labour: No one should be held in slavery or required to perform forced labour.

- The right to liberty and security: Everyone has the right not to be detained and deprived of their liberty, unless it is within the law, and the correct legal procedures are followed.

- The right to a fair trial: Everyone has the right to a fair trial and a public hearing within a reasonable period of time. Everyone charged with a criminal offence is presumed innocent, until proved guilty.

- No punishment without law: No one should be found guilty of an offence that was not a crime at the time it was committed.

- Right to respect a person's private and family life: Everyone has the right to respect for their private and family life, their home, and their correspondence. There should be no interference with this, unless for very good reasons, such as state security, public safety or the prevention of crime.

- Freedom of thought, conscience, and religion: Everyone is free to hold whatever views and beliefs they wish. Again this right will only be limited for reasons such as public safety, the protection of public order, and the protection of the rights and freedoms of others.

- Freedom of expression: Everyone has the freedom to express their views - but this may be limited for reasons of public safety or to protect the rights of others.

- Freedom of assembly and association: Everyone has the right to get together with other people in a peaceful way.

- Right to marry: Men and women have the right to marry and start a family, but our national law puts restrictions on when and with whom this may take place (see p. 134).

- Prohibition of discrimination: Everyone is entitled to the rights and freedoms set out in the European Convention on Human Rights, regardless of their race, sex, language, religion, political opinion, national or social origin.

- Protection of property: No one shall be deprived of their possessions, except in very limited circumstances, such as when the State can take money for payment of taxes or confiscate goods that are unlawful or pose some kind of danger.

- The right to education: No one shall be denied the right to education.

- The right to free elections: Elections for government must be free and fair and must take place by secret ballot.

- Prohibition of the death penalty: No one shall be condemned to death or executed.

Equal opportunities

For more than thirty years the law in Britain has gradually developed to try to make sure that people are not treated unfairly because of their sex, race or a disability. The law in this area is continually developing. For example, at the end of 2003 new regulations came into force protecting people who face discrimination at work because of their sexuality or their religion. In 2006 unfair age discrimination at work will also become unlawful.

Discrimination laws in the UK do not just apply to people at work. Race, sex, and disability discrimination in areas like education, housing, shopping and leisure are also against the law.

If you face problems of this kind, more information is available from the Citizens Advice Bureau or from one of the following organisations.

The Commission for Racial Equality, **www.cre.gov.uk**
The Equal Opportunities Commission, **www.eoc.org.uk**
The Disability Rights Commission, **www.drc.org.uk**

For further information on discrimination at work, see p. 111.

Racially and religiously motivated crime

In Britain it is a criminal offence to use abusive or insulting words in public in a way designed to cause people harassment, alarm or distress. Anyone who abuses, harasses, or attacks another person because of their religion or racial origin can be prosecuted. Courts now give people who commit racially or religiously motivated crimes increased penalties.

If you are the victim of, or witness such an attack, it is important to report it to the police. They have a duty to take action against such incidents. You may ask to be interviewed at the police station, at home, or at another location that is mutually convenient.

Further information and guidance on all these matters is available from the nearest Citizens Advice Bureau or Race Equality Council.

MARRIAGE AND DIVORCE
Marriage

In order to marry, each partner must be 16 years of age or over, and unmarried. Anyone aged 16 or 17 wishing to marry also needs their parents' written permission. Marriage between close blood relatives is forbidden. However marriage between cousins is permitted. No one can be forced to marry against their wishes, however strong the wishes of the family may be.

Engagement

Many couples show their intention to marry by announcing their engagement, and often the woman in particular will wear an engagement ring given to her by her fiancé. Many years ago an engagement was seen as a legal contract. Today it is not. If a person breaks off their engagement there is usually no duty even to return the ring. An engagement ring is seen as a gift, and may be kept, unless it was originally agreed to return it if the marriage did not take place.

Getting married

A marriage ceremony must almost always be held in a register office, a registered place of worship, or premises that have been approved by the local authority. A list of these can be obtained from the council offices or town hall.

In order to go through a marriage ceremony couples must first obtain Certificates from the Registrar of Marriages in the district(s) in which they live. Normally Certificates must be obtained at least 21 days, and not more than three months, before the proposed date of the wedding. Among the documents needed to obtain a Certificate for marriage is a birth certificate or, if this is not available, a personal identity document. If one of the partners has been married before, proof is required that this marriage has ended.

Further details about this and other formalities surrounding marriage are available from religious ministers who are authorised to conduct marriages and the local registrar of marriages, whose contact details can be found in the phone book under 'Registration of births, deaths & marriages.'

All marriage ceremonies, both religious and civil, stress the importance of marriage as a lifelong partnership. Partners have a duty to support and be faithful to one another.

It is customary in Britain for a married woman to take her husband's surname, but there is no legal duty to do this, and a number of women today keep the surname they had before they were married, and/or use it in their work.

Living together

In recent years, it has become increasingly common in Britain for couples to live together without marrying, or at least to delay their marriage for a number of years. Couples who live together without marrying do not have the same legal rights as those who are married.

Problems for unmarried couples can occur if a relationship breaks up. If, for example, only one partner's name is on the tenancy agreement or title deeds to their property, the other may find some difficulty in establishing their right to stay on in the property, or to claim a share in its value.

When a married person dies without making a will, their husband or wife is entitled to all or most of their possessions. This rule does not apply, however, to a couple that were not married. In these circumstances it can be very difficult for the surviving member to obtain any of their partner's possessions.

If an unmarried couple have a child, both parents have a duty to maintain that child until he or she reaches 18 years of age.

Same-sex partnerships

In November 2003, the Government announced plans to give same-sex partners similar legal rights to married couples, as they do in a number of other European countries. In order to receive these new entitlements, couples will be required to register their commitment in a civil ceremony.

Divorce

When a man or woman applies for a divorce they must prove to a court that their marriage has "irretrievably broken down". They can show this if one of the five following things has happened:

- their partner has committed adultery, and they have not by their behaviour condoned it,

- their partner has behaved unreasonably. This covers many things, such as assault, refusing to have children, being very anti-social,

- they have lived apart for two years and both want a divorce,

- they have lived apart for five years and only one partner wants a divorce,

- one partner has deserted the other for at least two years immediately before the application.

A divorce cannot take place within the first year of marriage.

Help and advice

The breakdown of a marriage can be difficult to cope with for all those involved. Family doctors are sometimes able to help in these circumstances, and can arrange for a patient to see a family therapist. There is also a long established voluntary independent organisation in Britain called Relate, which has counsellors specially trained to help people work through relationship difficulties. Contact details are available from the phone book, under "Relate" or at www.relate.org.uk

If you are in a position where you are facing divorce, or you have been deserted, it is essential to consult a solicitor for general advice before proceedings start about your legal position, particularly if you have young children, and there are disputes over money or property.

Domestic violence

Brutality in the home is as much a crime under UK law as any other form of violence. Anyone who is violent towards their partner - whether they are a woman or a man, married or living together - can be prosecuted for a serious offence such as assault, or grievous bodily harm. A husband who forces himself on his unwilling wife may be charged with rape.

If you are in this situation, it is important to get help as soon as possible. A solicitor or the Citizens Advice Bureau can explain the options that you have available to you. In many areas there are places of refuge, or shelters, for women in such difficulties. Emergency telephone numbers are listed in the Helpline section at the front of the Yellow Pages and, for women, the number of the nearest Women's Centre is in the phone book. The police can also help you find such a place.

CHILDREN
Parents' responsibilities

The law says that parents of a child who are *married* to one another have equal responsibility for their child. This continues if the parents later separate or divorce. However, when a child's parents are *not* married, only the mother has parental responsibility unless the father jointly registers the child's birth with the mother, subsequently marries the mother, obtains her agreement, or acquires parental responsibility by applying to a court. Parental responsibility continues until a child reaches the age of 18.

Support

Both parents, whether or not they are married to each other, have a legal responsibility to maintain their child financially. A father who does not have parental responsibility in law still has a duty to support his child financially.

When a parent is not living with, and failing to support their child, the other parent can apply to the Child Support Agency to assess the amount of money that the absent parent should pay. You can obtain more information from the Citizens Advice Bureau and the Child Support Agency Helpline, tel 08457 133 133.

Control

Parents are responsible for the care and control of their children. By law, they may use reasonable force to discipline them. But if this punishment is too severe, they may be prosecuted for assault, or the child may be taken into the care of the local authority.

Many voluntary organisations and local authorities offer parenting programmes, giving help and advice on being a parent. Information on many aspects of parenthood is also available on the BBC website, **www.bbc.co.uk/parenting**

Child protection

Every local authority has a legal duty to protect all children in its area from danger, and must place the interest of the child above all else. If it believes that a child is suffering significant harm at home, it must take action to try to stop this from happening.

As a rule, local authorities always try to work *with* parents, and there are a number of ways in which they do this. However local authorities do have the power to take a child out of its home and into care - although this is only done in an emergency or when all other possibilities have failed.

There are specific laws in Britain dealing with the employment of children (see p. 118).

Medical consultation and treatment

Once a young person reaches the age of sixteen they no longer need their parent's permission to agree to medical consultation or treatment, as long as the doctor or nurse believes that the young person fully understands what is involved.

When a young person *below* the age of sixteen seeks contraceptive advice and treatment the doctor will encourage them to discuss the matter with one or both of their parents. However most doctors who believe that a young person is able to understand what is involved will almost certainly prescribe contraception.

Leaving a child on their own

As a general rule, it is against the law for children to be left alone in a house unless they are in the care of a responsible person aged *sixteen* or over.

For information on registered childminders and childcare, see p. 111.

CONSUMER PROTECTION

No one can be certain that the goods they buy will be entirely trouble-free. However, certain things can be done to reduce the likelihood of problems.

❶ Be wary of advertisements that make exaggerated or tempting claims, and of people who try to sell you things on your doorstep.

❷ Keep the receipt you were given when you bought the item - particularly if the goods were expensive.

❸ If there is a problem with something you bought, stop using it straightaway and report the matter to the shop or trader as soon as possible. Make sure you have the receipt available as proof of purchase.

❹ If you have to make a complaint to the store or company, keep a note of the telephone calls you make, and copies of letters or e-mails that you send.

Goods and services

The prices of most new goods are clearly marked, and these are the prices that customers are expected to pay. Generally speaking, people in Britain rarely haggle over prices, although bargaining may take place when buying houses, second-hand goods and some household services.

Contract

When you buy something from a shop or pay for a service, you are making a legal contract with the store or the business providing the service. This means that, in return for the money that you pay, the item that you buy should do everything that you can reasonably expect and, in particular all that the seller and manufacturer claim.

The law covering most of the everyday things that we buy is the *Sale of Goods Act 1979*. It states that goods you buy from a shop or trader must:

- be of satisfactory quality, and

- match the description, and

- be fit for all their intended purposes.

Satisfactory quality

This means that goods must be free from faults and not scratched or damaged - unless the fault was pointed out by the sales assistant or you inspected the item when you bought it and had plenty of opportunity to discover the fault.

The rule applies to goods bought in a sale and those bought second-hand, from a shop or trader. It does not however apply to those bought from a private individual, for example through an advertisement in the paper, where the buyer is expected to take responsibility for the quality of goods that they buy.

Match the description

Goods that you buy must be the same as the description on the packaging or advertisement given at the time of the sale. This rule applies to all goods sold - including second-hand goods sold privately.

Fit for all their intended purposes

This means that the goods must do what the seller, packaging or advertising claims.

Services

The law covering services - such as hairdressing or shoe repairs - states that services must be done:

- with reasonable care and skill, and

- within a reasonable time, and

- for a reasonable charge

Problems are less likely to occur if certain things are agreed before the work is started, such as the cost, the amount of time it will take, and what happens if there is a particular problem.

Mail order and Internet shopping

There are special regulations protecting people who buy goods from home, by post, phone, or on the Internet. As well as the rights listed above, you are also entitled to cancel your order within seven working days if you change your mind and decide that you no longer want the goods. Certain items, however, are excluded from this. These include bookings for tickets or accommodation, items like audio and video recordings that have been opened, newspapers, magazines, and perishable items, such as flowers or food.

You are also entitled to a full refund if the goods are not provided by the date agreed or within 30 days if no time was specified.

When buying goods over the Internet it is advisable to make sure you have the trader's full address and that the website offers a secure way of paying, shown by a small picture of padlock at the bottom of the screen.

Complaints

If the fault appears shortly after you bought the goods and you haven't misused them, you are entitled to your money back (or, if you choose, a replacement, if available). The assistant may tell you that the item will have to be repaired or sent back to the manufacturer. However, the contract that you made when you bought the goods was with the shop, and not the manufacturer. This means that it is the shop's responsibility to deal with faults, and not the manufacturer's. In these circumstances, therefore, you have every right to ask for your money back.

If the item worked well at first, and then developed a fault, you may still be entitled to some or all of your money back, to be offered a replacement, or to have it repaired free of charge. It all depends on how long you have had the goods, the seriousness of the fault, and whether it is unreasonable for a fault to develop so soon.

Paying by credit card

If you are not satisfied with something costing between £100-£30,000 that you bought by credit card, you can claim the money back instead from the credit card company. This can be useful if the trader ignores your complaints or has gone out of business.

Help and advice

Advice is available locally from the Citizens Advice Bureau and the Trading Standards Office, whose telephone number and address are listed in the phone book under the name of your local council.

Which? is an independent magazine giving a guide to the price and performance of many products. The magazine is available on subscription, and copies are usually available in the reference department of most public libraries.

More information about consumer rights is available from the BBC Website, **www.bbc.co.uk**, and the Office of Fair Trading. This is the government's official watchdog, protecting consumer interests, **www.oft.gov.uk**

CRIMINAL COURTS

The court system in Scotland and Northern Ireland is different from that in England and Wales. The information below applies to England and Wales only.

Magistrates' court

All criminal cases are first brought to a magistrates' court, where most of them are dealt with. Some cases are referred to the Crown Court; see below.

Magistrates, also known as justices of the peace, are members of the local community. They work unpaid and have no legal qualifications. They do, however, receive training for their work as a magistrate.

Crown Court

More serious offences are tried in the Crown Court, which is presided over by a judge. A jury, however, reaches the verdict in the case. The jury is made up of twelve members of the public, chosen at random from the local electoral register (see p. 73).

Certain people - particularly those whose work is connected with the law - may not serve on a jury, and certain others are automatically excused if they wish. However, anyone else called for service on a jury must attend, unless they can show good reason why they may be excused.

Youth court

If the accused is aged 17 or under, the case will normally be heard in a youth court in front of three specially trained magistrates.

The parents of the young person are expected to attend the case - and must do so if the accused is under 16 - but members of the public are not admitted, nor can the identity or pictures of the young person concerned be published in the press or other media.

CIVIL COURTS
County courts

County courts, located in most towns and cities, deal with a wide range of civil disputes. These include people trying to recover money that they are owed, cases involving personal injury, family matters, breaches of contract and divorce.

The small claims procedure

This is an informal way of settling disputes, designed to save people time and money, by allowing them to conduct their case without using a solicitor. Cases usually involve claims of less than £5,000. The hearing is held in an ordinary room and the setting is much less formal than a normal court. The judge does not wear a wig or gown and both sides are seated around a table. Details about this procedure are available from local county court, under 'Courts' in the phone book.

Tribunals

Separate tribunals rather than courts hear certain areas of dispute, such as employment, rent, land use, immigration, and Child Support.

LEGAL ADVICE AND AID
Solicitors

Solicitors are trained lawyers who give advice on legal matters, take action on their client's behalf, and represent them in court. There are solicitors' offices in every town and city in England and Wales. Many advertise in local papers and the Yellow Pages, often indicating those aspects of law in which they specialise.

Although solicitors are trained to deal with a wide range of legal problems, it is important that your solicitor has the right experience to help you with your case. The Citizens Advice Bureau can give you the names of local solicitors who specialise in particular areas of law, as can the Law Society, tel 020 7242 1222, **www.solicitors-online.com**, and the Community Legal Service, tel 0845 608 1222, **www.justask.org.uk**

Costs

Solicitors normally charge clients on the basis of the amount of time they spend on their case. It is very important to find out at the start how much your case is likely to cost and how it would be financed.

Financial help or legal aid

A person questioned or charged in connection with a *crime* is entitled to free advice from a duty solicitor (see p.131), and free representation by a solicitor on their first appearance in court. Help may also be available with the costs of any further appearances in court, although this will depend on the nature of the case and the income and savings of the defendant, on which a solicitor can advise.

For *civil* cases, schemes are available covering the cost of help and advice from a solicitor, and representation in court. However not all types of cases are covered and help is available only to those whose income and savings are below a certain level. Again a solicitor can advise on eligibility. Help with the cost of civil legal action is harder to obtain now than it was in the past. Costs may instead be paid by the client, or on a 'no win, no fee' basis.

'No win, no fee' refers to cases in which the solicitor charges the client a fee only if they win their case. Although this can sound very attractive to a client, there are likely to be a number of hidden costs. For example, although clients do not have to pay their own costs if they lose, they will often have to pay those of the other side. As always, it is important to obtain a written estimate of all charges at the outset, and to make sure you fully understand what it all means.

Law Centres

There are Law Centres in a number of major cities, staffed by qualified lawyers who can give advice and possibly take on a case in much the same way as a solicitor. The Law Centres Federation, tel 020 7387 8570, **www.lawcentres.org.uk**, can give you the address of your nearest Centre.

Other advice and information

Citizens Advice Bureaux with offices in most towns and cities can provide free information and confidential advice on all kinds of legal problems (see p. 122). They also have an information website, **www.adviceguide.org.uk**, which gives up-to-date information on a wide range of legal problems in English, Welsh, Bengali, Chinese, Gujarati, Punjabi and Urdu.

Just Ask!

This is the website of the Community Legal Service, which provides online information in seven languages on a wide range of legal questions, and can indicate solicitors, advice agencies and other information providers in your area whom you can contact for advice and help.

For teenagers

The *Young Citizen's Passport* is a widely used and down-to-earth practical guide to everyday law produced by the Citizenship Foundation and written specially for the needs of young people aged 14-19. Three different editions are available covering the law in England and Wales, Scotland and Northern Ireland. To order a copy and for further details, order through any bookshop or contact the publishers Hodder Murray, tel 020 7873 6372.